5 Traits
of a
Healthy
Family

5 Traits of a Healthy Family

STEPS YOU
CAN TAKE TO

•

GROW CLOSER

•

COMMUNICATE
BETTER

•

& CHANGE
THE WORLD

•

TOGETHER

of a Healthy Family

Gary Chapman

with Derek Chapman

NORTHFIELD PUBLISHING

CHICAGO

Edited by Avrie Roberts
Interior design: Ragont Design
Cover design: Erik M. Peterson
Cover illustration number five © 2023 by evseev_tim/Adobe Stock (502355806). All rights reserved.
Author photo: P.S. Photography

Library of Congress Cataloging-in-Publication Data

Names: Chapman, Gary D., 1938- author.
Title: 5 traits of a healthy family : steps you can take to grow closer,
    communicate better, and change the world together / Gary Chapman with
    Derek Chapman.
Other titles: Five signs of a loving family | Five traits of a healthy
    family
Description: Chicago : Northfield Publishing, [2023] | "Previously
    published as Five Signs of a Loving Family and The Family You've Always
    Wanted"--Verso. | Includes bibliographical references. | Summary: "What
    are the five timeless characteristics that create a healthy family?
    Through personal stories, Gary teaches about husbands and wives who love
    one another; husbands who love, support, and lead; families who serve;
    parents who guide; and children who obey and honor. A free online
    resource accompanies this book"-- Provided by publisher.
Identifiers: LCCN 2023004506 (print) | LCCN 2023004507 (ebook) | ISBN
    9780802429742 | ISBN 9780802473455 (ebook)
Subjects: LCSH: Families--United States--Psychological aspects. |
    Communication in families--United States. | BISAC: RELIGION / Christian
    Living / Family & Relationships | FAMILY & RELATIONSHIPS / Parenting /
    General
Classification: LCC HQ536 .C435 2023 (print) | LCC HQ536 (ebook) | DDC
    306.850973--dc23/eng/20230309
LC record available at https://lccn.loc.gov/2023004506
LC ebook record available at https://lccn.loc.gov/2023004507

We hope you enjoy this book from Northfield Publishing. Our goal is to provide high-quality, thought-provoking books and products that connect truth to your real needs and challenges. For more information on other books and products that will help you with all your important relationships, go to northfieldpublishing.com or write to:

Northfield Publishing
820 N. LaSalle Boulevard
Chicago, IL 60610

1 3 5 7 9 10 8 6 4 2

Printed in the United States of America

Dedicated to Karolyn and Shelley

Contents

Introduction

I've been in the family business for more than forty-five years. Not just my own family but thousands of others have walked through the doors of my office and expressed the joys and sorrows of family. Few things in life have as much potential for bringing us happiness as do family relationships. Conversely, few things can bring us as much pain as broken family relationships. I have heard literally thousands of women and men share their heart's desire for the family they've always wanted.

But how, especially in today's culture, can we achieve that heart's desire?

In recent years, I have had a growing awareness that many in our day have no clear picture of a healthy family. They know the pain and problems of a dysfunctional family, but they do not know what a healthy family would look like. Thus, I felt compelled to write this book.

To say that the family in Western culture is in trouble is an understatement. It is more realistic to say that the family has lost its way. In our time the very definition of "family" has been challenged, as has the concept of the family—husband, wife, usually children—as the foundational building block of society. The family has been bombarded with influences ranging from the lure of "bigger, better, more" to our culture's emphasis on personal happiness above all else. Young people forming families today often lack models for healthy relationships.

I have been a student of the family for more than forty years, beginning as a student of anthropology with a special emphasis on family structure. I have been at the business of helping people professionally with marriage and family struggles for more than forty-five years. My wife, Karolyn, and I raised a son, Derek, and daughter, Shelley, both now grown with families of their own. Their influence and insights have added immeasurably to this book.

I have concluded that there are five elements essential to building a healthy family, so you will find this book divided into five sections that explore each of these. In addition, in the digital resource "The Family Adventure Guide" you will find practical ideas for immediately applying these insights to your own family—to help you grow into the family you always wanted. What happens to your family will affect the nation, even the world, for better or for worse. We rise or fall together. I hope that these traits of a healthy family will be helpful to you.

—GARY CHAPMAN

An Outsider in the Family

Years ago, a young man recently graduated from college and teaching in a local high school approached me with a shocking question: "Would you and your wife allow me to move into your house for a year and observe your family in operation?" He said that he had grown up in an unhealthy family and in college had found a measure of healing through a Christian group on the university campus. Nevertheless, he had no idea what a healthy marriage and family was like. He had read some books on family life, but he wanted to see a healthy family in action. Would we integrate him into our family for a year and give him that experience?

To say the least, I was taken aback by the idea. It was not a request I had ever had before or since. I responded as every wise and mature counselor would respond: "Let me think about it." My first internal, emotional response was, *This will never work.* We lived in a small three-bedroom, two-bathroom house at the time. We had two small children—all the bedrooms were occupied, and we were already running into each other in the bathrooms. How could we bring in an outsider, especially an adult? Second, I wondered, *How would this affect our family?* An outsider gazing at us, and analyzing what we are doing and how we relate to each other. Wouldn't we start "playing to the camera"? Wouldn't we become unreal?

I had been on enough anthropology field trips to know that the presence of the anthropologist who moves into the tribal village to study the culture does, in fact, affect the culture (although you don't read much about this in the anthropologists' reports). Initially his presence is the news of the decade or the event of a lifetime. This person has come into the village, making strange sounds and motions. He obviously is not one of us. Why is he here? Should we eat him and thank the gods for bringing us an easy meal? Or should we pamper him and see if he knows about some new hunting grounds where game is plentiful?

Now here was a young man asking to move into my village and observe. Well, at least he spoke my language, and he communicated his purpose. I certainly had an advantage over the villagers who sometimes take months to figure out why this strange person who asks such foolish questions and makes odd markings on white mats has come to live in their village.

"DO WE HAVE SOMETHING WORTH SHARING?"

Being a part of a loving family, I discussed this strange request with my wife and two children. Wouldn't you know it—they liked the idea. Shelley and Derek thought it would be great to have an older brother, and Karolyn, who is always into the "not so usual" kind of things, thought it would be a good experiment. "Maybe it would help this young man the rest of his life, and maybe a little sharing of our family would be good for us. Haven't we always taught the children 'It is more blessed to give than to receive'?" (I've never liked the way she takes the lofty principles we teach the children and applies them to my life.)

"What about a bedroom?" I asked.

"We will build a wall in the basement and make a room and closet. It's just open wasted space—no problem." The children suggested that he could share their bathroom. Easy for them to say—they used our bathroom half the time already. I could see it now—all four of us using one bathroom while the outsider used the other. (Why am I so inclined to believe the worst?)

I asked myself, "Do we have something worth sharing?" I remembered the words of family expert Edith Schaeffer: "If a family is to be really shared, then there needs to be something to share."[1] In other words, before you can bring another person into your family, you must first of all be a functioning family. I could honestly say that I believed that we had a pretty healthy family. We weren't perfect. We had been through many struggles, especially when Karolyn and I were first married, before the children came. But we learned much through these struggles and were now enjoying the fruit of hard work. Yes, we had something to pass on.

"EMBRACED BY YOUR FAMILY"

So, we did. We built the wall across one end of the basement, creating a bedroom, and installed draw doors on one end of the room, creating a closet. We then cut a hole in the metal ductwork and inserted a heat and air vent, and moved in a used bed and nightstand from my mother's attic. Then John moved in.

We all agreed that John would be a part of our family for the next year, and we would try to be as "normal" as possible. John saw it all, heard it all, was a part of it all. Years later, he wrote,

> Looking back on that experience, I have many pleasant memories. I remember walking past Shelley early in the morning as she practiced the piano. I remember washing the dishes and realizing for the first time how slow and deliberate I was. The humor of whenever Karolyn would want them done fast, she would do it and get it done in five minutes to my

twenty minutes since I was such a perfectionist. I remember the warm images of being at the dinner table and just being embraced by the family in a very appropriate and loving way. I remember the joy of Fridays when after dinner, college students would come over for discussions. Those were great evenings. The lingering memories are of being in your home and being part of that comfortable, healthy, positive environment. Virtually every other time in my life before that was dysfunctional. After that, I grew increasingly into what I think is a fairly responsible, healthy person.

What we sought to pass on to John by this live-in experience, I want to try to communicate to you in written form. I'll try to be vivid enough that you can smell some of the smells and feel some of the emotions that we all experienced. I'll also illustrate some of these principles by the lives of many other families who have been kind enough to discuss their lives with me through the years. Hopefully Derek's poems will help you enter into the experience. Here are his reflections on an outsider in our midst.

> *A stranger's eyes on us*
> *Looking at and through us*
> *As morning light falls through*
> *Windows onto breakfast table*
> *We pause for prayer—*
> *His eyes stay open, watching*
> *To see if it is real—this*
> *Family bowing over another meal.*

PART ONE

Families Who Serve

CHAPTER ONE

From Pain to Pleasure

A PERSONAL JOURNEY

What was John to discover in our family? I hoped he would observe people who cared about serving—both one another and beyond.

This had been the first step, taken years earlier, in turning our marriage from withering to thriving. I entered marriage with the idea that my wife would make me supremely happy, that she would satisfy my deep yearnings for companionship and love. To be sure, I intended to make her happy as well, but most of my dreams focused on how happy *I* would be when we were married.

Six months after marriage, I was more miserable than I had been in twenty-three years. Before marriage, I dreamed about how happy I would be—now my dream had become a nightmare. I discovered all sorts of things I did not know before we were married. In the months before we were married, I dreamed about what it would be like at night in our apartment. I could visualize the two of us sitting in our little apartment. I would be at the desk studying (I was in graduate school), and she would be sitting on the couch. When I got tired of studying, I would lift my eyes, our eyes would meet, and there would be warm vibes between the two of us. After we got married, I discovered that my wife did not want to sit on the couch and watch me study. If I was going to study, she wanted to go downstairs and visit people in the apartment complex, make new friends, and use her time socializing. I sat in our little apartment alone thinking, *This is what it was like before we got married*; the only difference was that I was in a dorm room, much cheaper than this place. Instead of warm vibes, I felt the ache of loneliness.

Before marriage, I dreamed that every night about 10:30, we would go to bed together. Ahh—going to bed with a woman every night at 10:30. What pleasure! After we got married, I discovered that it had never crossed her mind to go to bed with *anybody* at 10:30 every night. Her ideal was to come up from visiting about 10:30 and read a book till midnight. I was thinking, *Why didn't you read your book while I read my book?* Then we could go to bed together.

Before we got married, I thought that every morning when the sun gets up, everybody gets up. After we were married, I found out that my wife didn't do mornings. It didn't take me long not to like her, and it didn't take her long not to like me. We succeeded in being utterly miserable. In time, we both wondered why we had married each other. We seemed to disagree on everything. We were different in every way. The distance between us mounted, and our differences became divisive. The dream was gone, and the grief was intense.

TURNING WAR INTO PEACE

Our first approach was an effort toward mutual annihilation. I freely pointed out her faults, and she mine. We succeeded in wounding each other regularly. I knew that my ideas were logical and that if she would listen to me, we could have a good marriage. She perceived that my ideas were out of touch with reality and that if I would listen to her, we could find a meeting place. We both became preachers without an audience. Our sermons fell on deaf ears, and our pain compounded.

Our marriage did not turn around overnight. No magic wand was waved. Our marriage began to turn around over the period of about a year, several years into the marriage. It began to dawn on me that I had approached our marriage with a very conceited, self-centered attitude. I had really believed that if she would listen to me and do what I wanted, we would both be happy; that if she would make me happy, I would somehow see that it was reciprocated. I had the idea that whatever made me happy would automatically make her happy. I find it hard to admit, but I spent little time thinking about her well-being. My focus was on my own pain and unmet needs and desires.

My search for an answer to our painful dilemma led me to a reexamination of the life and teachings of Jesus. The stories I had heard as a child about His healing the sick, feeding the hungry, and speaking with kindness and hope to the destitute flooded my mind. As an adult, I now wondered if I had overlooked profound truth in those simple accounts. With twenty-seven hours of academic studies in the Greek language behind me, I decided that I would explore the life and teachings of Jesus in the original documents. What I discovered could have been discovered in a simple reading of the English text. His life and teachings focused on sacrificial service to others. He once said, "I did not come to be served, but to serve." It is a theme that all truly great men and women of the past have affirmed. Life's greatest meaning is not found in getting but in giving. Could this profound principle make a significant difference in my marriage? I was determined to find out.

LESS PREACHING, MORE DOING

How would a wife respond to a husband who sincerely sought to serve her? To discover her needs and desires and to seek to fulfill them? I began quietly and slowly to do some of the things she had requested in the past. By now, we were too estranged to talk about our relationship, but I could choose to take action on some of her previous complaints. I started washing dishes without being asked. I volunteered to fold the laundry. It seemed to me these were the kinds of things Jesus might have done had He been married. When she made specific requests, I determined to respond cheerfully and, if possible, to do them. In less than three months, Karolyn's attitude toward me began to change. She came out of her shell of withdrawal and began to talk again. I think she sensed that my days of preaching were over and that my attitude toward life was changing.

In due time, I found her doing little things that I had requested in the past. She held my hand as we walked in public, she smiled when I tried to make a joke, she touched me as she walked by my desk. Before long, our hostility was gone, and we began to feel positive feelings toward each other. I remember the first day I had the thought, *Maybe I could love her again.* For months, I had had no feelings of love, but only pain, hurt, anger, hostility. Now, all that seemed to be gone, and it was replaced by warm feelings. I found myself thinking that I wouldn't mind touching her again if I thought she'd let me. I wasn't about to ask her, but I thought, *I wouldn't mind if she wouldn't mind.* Before spring the thought had become reality. Romantic feelings were reborn and sexual intimacy, which seemed so far away, had become reality. We had come full circle. We were no longer enemies preaching at each other; we had become sensitive to each other's desires. Our attitudes had become that of serving rather than demanding. And we were reaping the benefit of intimacy.

All of that had happened in what seems now a distant past. Now, here we were with two children and an outsider. We had sought to teach our children what we believed to be one of the most important ingredients of a healthy family—an attitude of service. Would John observe it? Could it be discovered by observation? I sincerely hoped so.

CHAPTER TWO

How Families Serve

When I first began to lead marriage and family workshops, we used a Friday night to Saturday format. I would ask couples to bring a sack lunch on Saturdays. I would often ask, at the end of the Friday night session, "Who would like to bring me a lunch tomorrow?" Immediately three or four hands shot up.

Why do these people freely and spontaneously volunteer to bring a lunch to a stranger? Chances are they learned the attitude of service as children. They are eager to serve, and they find satisfaction in helping others. In a loving family, this attitude of service will permeate the entire family. Family members will serve each other, and they will serve beyond the family structure.

Cultural critic and bestselling author Bill Bennett lists "work" as one of the top ten virtues.[1] And the Bible is full of teachings and examples of diligence and effort—the book of Proverbs alone has dozens of verses addressing work (and laziness). Most historians agree that Western culture was built on the work ethic. Work is defined as physical and mental exertion toward the accomplishment of some worthy goal. And work starts in the home.

CAN SOMEBODY TAKE OUT THE TRASH?

In the family, much work needs to be done. Clothes must be washed, folded, and perhaps ironed. Beds need to be made, food has to be prepared or purchased and served (does anyone still cook?). There is trash to be stashed, floors to be vacuumed or swept or mopped. Cars need oil changes, bills have to be paid, clutter cleaned up, pets cared for. Even with today's smaller yards, someone still needs to mow the lawn, run the leaf blower, or trim the bushes.

The list goes on. The work never seems to end. We may not have as much work today as in the frontier days, and many people hire help, but there's still plenty of work to go around. With most husbands and more than 50 percent of wives working outside the home, parents have limited time to get it all done.

Who will do the work? Hopefully, the family—all the family. In any sized family, there is enough work to go around. "The more the merrier," the old saying goes, but it is usually also true "The more the messier." John's coming into our family brought more clothes to be washed, more food to be prepared, etc. But it also brought another worker into the pool.

If work is such a fundamental virtue, then every family member should certainly learn to work. Some busy families neglect this responsibility, thinking it's more important for the kids to pursue activities like sports than it is for them to do chores. Or, the parents reason, "It's easier to do it myself." But we aren't doing our children any favors by letting them off the hook. We can delegate age-appropriate jobs, along with basic training on how to do the job. When our son, Derek, got to the lawn-mowing stage (which, incidentally, is my favorite stage of childrearing), he always wanted to mow back and forth. For years, I had mowed the grass in squares, starting at the outside and working my way to the middle, which left the trimmings in a nice tiny square in the middle of the yard—easy to bag. I explained my efficient strategy to Derek, but it never took. He developed a different philosophy—scatter the trimmings, and you don't have to bag. His back-and-forth pattern left light trimmings across the lawn that in twenty-four hours were hardly visible. I wrestled, trying to decide what was more important: my perfectionistic, efficient method or his creativity—his individuality. I opted for the latter. I refused to make him a robot or a clone, and that's hard for a perfectionistic parent.

Perhaps you are thinking, *So there is work to be done, and every family member needs to share the load. What's new?* "An attitude of service" is far more than simply getting the work done. In a healthy family, members have the sense that as I do something for the benefit of other family members, I am doing something genuinely good. Individuals have an internal desire to serve and an emotional sense of satisfaction with a job done for others. In a highly functional family, there develops the sense that service to others is one of life's highest callings.

A healthy family has an attitude of service to each other and to the world outside the walls of the family. Read the biographies of men and women who have lived lives of sacrificial service to others, and you will find that most of them grew up in families that nurtured the idea of service as virtuous.

Writer Philip Yancey notes that toward the end of his life, Albert Einstein removed the portraits of two scientists—Newton and Maxwell—from his wall. He replaced those with portraits of Gandhi and Schweitzer. Einstein explained that it was time to replace the image of success with the image of service.[2]

KIDS WHO WANT TO HELP, TEENS WHO WANT TO SERVE

An attitude of service is relatively easy to foster in the emerging child. As a baby becomes a toddler, she becomes a full-time explorer. In time, the explorer becomes a builder, and by the time the child is four, the builder has become a helper. The idea of service seems almost innate. If the child is allowed to help and affirmed for helping, he or she will likely be a willing worker well into the first and second grade. In grades three through six, a child's attitude of service will be greatly influenced by the models in the family. If the parents have talked about service as a virtue and have helped the child discover ways to serve family members, and if the child is given verbal affirmation for such acts of service, the child will continue to find satisfaction in serving well into adolescence.

In the wonderful years of thirteen to eighteen, there will be dramatic changes. If the teenager has internalized an attitude of service, he or she will reach out in many ways beyond the family circle. At school and perhaps at church, such teenagers will tend to be servant leaders. They will spend considerable time helping others achieve. But they may not be as eager to serve at home. They will likely spend more and more time away from the family and may even show resistance to family activities.

They are experiencing another of life's great urges—the urge to be free. The whole point is to put distance between the parents and the teen, space to grow toward independence. Doors to their rooms will be closed rather than open (actually a wonderful idea to a perfectionist parent). They are getting involved in activities away from home. The opinion of friends may be more important than the opinion of parents.

All of this distance and reluctance to continue in the service mode at home often creates conflicts in the family. But conflicts are not symptoms of disease; how we deal with conflicts will reveal the health of the family. In a loving family, conflicts are expected. We recognize that people do not always think and feel the same way. Certainly, parents and teens will not see the world out of the same eyes. Thus, we should not be surprised when conflict arises.

Healthy families learn how to process conflicts. Rather than avoiding the issues, we seek to put the issues on the table. Teens are encouraged to give their point of view while the parents listen. Parents genuinely seek to understand what the teen is feeling as well as what the teen is saying. Conversely, the teen listens to the parents' viewpoint with understanding ears. (Does this really happen in some families? Yes. It happens where there is a high level of security in the family.)

Contrary to some current thinking, teens really do want limits. "Is there anyone who stands for anything anymore?" a fifteen-year-old young man asked. "Everyone seems to accept anything, given the right situation. I wish adults gave us more guidance. Haven't they learned something during their life that would help us avoid some potholes?" Limits create boundaries, and boundaries give feelings of security. Security creates an atmosphere where teens can learn and grow. Thus, when the teen hits the stage of freedom seeking and may begin to forget the serving role in the family, parents must respect his or her desire to be independent but remind the teen that people are always interdependent and that serving others is a necessary part not only of family life but of all life.

Adults and youth alike are attracted to the young man or woman who goes out of his or her way to serve others. A number of years ago when I was directing the college outreach ministry of our church, I encountered four young men who attended the University of North Carolina. They had secured summer jobs in our city and had begun attending some of our activities for college students. I later discovered that they were all living in one small apartment with a view to saving as much money as possible during the summer. They had been attending activities only a couple of weeks when all four of them approached me and one of their more verbal members told me that they had decided to "plug into" our church for the summer and they wanted to offer their services. They would be happy to serve in any capacity I might suggest. Assuming that they were like many college students in those days, always thinking about the résumé, I thought they were volunteering for leadership positions in our summer programs. After all, "Volunteer Director" of the Building Bridges to Youth program would certainly impress a future employer.

I expressed appreciation for their volunteer spirit but informed them that we had to plan our summer programs in the winter and that all of our places of volunteer leadership were already assigned. Their friendly spokesman quickly responded, "No, no. We're not interested in leadership positions; we're talking about service."

"Can you give me some examples of what you have in mind?" I inquired.

Without hesitation, he said, "We were thinking that perhaps you could use someone to wash the dishes after the Wednesday evening meal or perhaps clean the ovens or mop the floors. Anything," he said. "We just want to serve."

"Oh, well, in that case," I said, "I think we have plenty of openings." Throughout that summer not only did they wash dishes, clean ovens, and mop floors, but they also washed buses, trimmed grass, and cleaned bathrooms. The people who were active in our church that summer have never forgotten "the boys from Carolina." In fact, their "attitude of service" affected the whole direction of our college ministry from that summer forward.

Not all service will be directed toward persons. For example, many young people love helping animals. Elizabeth, a junior high student, told me of her passion for helping troubled animals. I found her by a community lake putting a splint on a duck's leg. The duck had been hit by a passing car, and Elizabeth came to the rescue. All of us are impressed and encouraged by young people who "adopt" a section of highway or become involved in efforts to alleviate poverty in Africa. Such young people typically learned their attitude of service in the home.

HOW ADULTS SERVE

The independence of adulthood is often the soil out of which genuine service to others grows. Adults choose to have children, knowing that such a choice means twenty-four months of diapers, five years of bathing, two years of nursing or bottle-feeding, spoon-feeding, putting on 308 Band-Aids (with some kids, at least that many each year), attending a minimum of 220 ball games, cooking countless meals, sacrificing to pay college tuition, and a thousand other acts of service. Yet we choose—freely choose—children. And some couples often choose to adopt a child whom someone else is unable to serve.

Service to others is the highest pinnacle humanity ever scales. Most people who have studied His life closely agree that Jesus Christ stood on the pinnacle of greatness when He took a washbasin and towel and performed a lowly act of washing His disciples' feet. He removed all doubt as to His intent when He said, "Now that I, your Lord and Teacher, have washed your feet, you also should wash one another's feet. I have set you an example that you should do as I have done for you. . . . Now that you know these things, you will be blessed if you do them."[3] On another occasion, He told His followers that "whoever wants to become great among you must be your servant."[4]

It's a great paradox—the way up is down. True greatness is expressed in serving, not in dominating. No parents challenge their children to be like Hitler, while thousands continue to challenge their children to be like Jesus. Service is a mark of greatness.

What did John, our live-in anthropologist, observe in our family? He saw Karolyn, who is definitely not a morning person, getting up five days a week and cooking a hot breakfast for the family—an act of service on the level of Mother Teresa. (If you are a morning person, you will not understand this.) This morning sacrifice was not born out of compulsion. It was not something I demanded, or even expected, though I unashamedly enjoyed it. As Shelley, our firstborn, reached school age, Karolyn came up with the idea that children needed a hot breakfast before school and that this would be one of her ways of serving the family. She saw it as a means of expressing gratitude to God for the gift of children. It was, I think, a noble expression of her attitude of service.

In twelve years, Shelley went off to college just as Derek entered high school. The hot breakfast continued four more years until the day Derek said good-bye and headed out to stretch his mind with philosophy, English, and religious studies. Then an era ended as quietly as it had begun sixteen years earlier. I went back to cold cereal, grapefruit, and bananas, which by that time was much better for me. Even now when the children come home from their adult pursuits, they talk about those hot breakfasts and what a pleasant memory they are. The memory is sustained once a year when, on Christmas morning, Karolyn again goes to the kitchen and repeats that ancient ritual of service.

What effect did all this have on John? This is what he said years later:

I don't think I appreciated it as much then as I do now, being older and having a keener sense of the sacrifice in the family, but from what I personally experienced, you made me a part of the family. I didn't feel like a boarder. I didn't feel like an afterthought or an appendage. I felt like I was part of the family. I looked up to you and Karolyn almost in a fatherly-motherly way. I felt like I was an older brother to Shelley and to Derek. In a larger sense, there was a sacrificial attitude in your allowing me to come into your family. Because it is an intrusion, it introduces a different dynamic into the household. I didn't have any sense of the cost of that then. I always felt like you and Karolyn had time for me whenever I wanted to talk about anything. You both were extremely busy and active, but I always felt that there was free accessibility and I never felt that it was an imposition for me to be spending time talking with you. I remember Christmas, Shelley and Derek giving me a present, and that was very neat. I saw the family serving each other.

In a healthy family, this attitude of the value of helping others serves as the oil that lubricates the wheels of family life. Without it, the wheels run down, and family life stalls. With it, a family flourishes. Derek captures something of the climate that is created by acts of service.

The Service of Love

On this morning in my memory
I hear melody-chimes hanging
from the doorway to their bedroom.
Something singing before we awake—
It is the Carolina sky breaking through
my window. Outside
the dogs and squirrels jostle
the eye of morning open.
Half awake, I hear
the distant voice of mother
making the miracle of bacon, biscuit;
the fragrances of day
call from the kitchen.
Father's tender palms already
scanning for today's breakfast truth,
Sister fingering Chopin's scales
into the sleeping heart of brother.
And the rumbling flash of mother
raising the melody of sizzling bacon,

scrambled eggs, rising biscuits
to a new pitch—
the pain of arising early to feed
half-opened mouths, to feed still
half-opened hearts, to slowly,
through simple and painful morning,
awaken gifts in us, call forth in us
this lasting chorus.

For more information on how you and your family can develop an attitude of service, see the code on page 177 to access the Family Adventure Guide at **www.5lovelanguages.com/5traits**. This guide is to help put into practice the healthy traits discussed in this book. You'll find a number of assessments, things to think about, and opportunities for deeper discussion.

PART TWO

Husbands and Wives Who Relate Intimately

CHAPTER THREE

Our Longing for Closeness

When we said "I DO," we put our names on the dotted line because we wanted to join our lives in a common dream of happiness. We intended to keep the open, caring relationship that emerged from our dating experience. In short, we expected *intimacy.* However, for many couples, when the emotional high of the "in love" obsession fades, intimacy becomes elusive. Many even find that they have different ideas on what intimacy is all about.

I had almost finished the second counseling session with a couple when the husband looked at me and said, "If we could get our sex life straightened out, everything else would be fine, but when we don't have sex, I feel that she doesn't care for me at all, and I can't go on like this forever." There, he had said it. It was on the table. I knew he felt relieved. As a counselor, I felt encouraged that he was openly expressing his need for sexual intimacy.

In both sessions, his wife had been saying things like, "We don't ever do anything together anymore; he is always gone. We used to do things together. Our communication is almost nonexistent. We don't ever talk. He doesn't understand my feelings. When I try to share my struggles, he gives me a quick answer and walks out of the room." She was crying for emotional intimacy.

The fact that they were in my office indicated that they had an intense concern for their marriage. They knew that things were not right between them. In reality, both of them wanted intimacy, but they were focusing on different aspects of intimacy: he, on physical intimacy, and she, on emotional intimacy. Such differences are not uncommon. The tragedy is that many couples have spent years condemning each other for not providing the intimacy they desire and have failed in learning how to create such intimacy. This section is designed to help you understand the extreme importance of marital intimacy and to give you practical ways to attain it.

"BONE OF MY BONES"

The English word for intimacy comes from the Latin word *intimus*, meaning "inner." Thus, intimacy involves two people opening their inner selves to each other. It is entering into each other's lives emotionally, intellectually, socially, physically, and spiritually. It is connecting at the deepest possible level in every area of life. Intimacy is accompanied by a sense of love and trust. We believe that the other person has our best interests in mind; thus, we can open ourselves up without fear that what we are telling or allowing to be seen will be used against us.

The desire for intimacy between a man and a woman is as old as the human race. The book of Genesis shows God creating woman from a portion of man's rib. When the man awoke from a deep sleep and saw the woman that God had created he said, "This is now bone of my bones and flesh of my flesh; she shall be called 'woman,' for she was taken out of man."[1] There she stood—another like him but with unique differences, more like him than anything he had seen and yet obviously different, separate from him and yet related to him. Something deep within him responded to something deep within her. This was no superficial encounter. It was deep responding unto deep. This was the heart of humanity responding to another human heart, another who was closer to him than all else in the universe.

These two realities, similarity and difference, are the raw material of human intimacy. Without these two, there could be no intimacy. Men and women are distinct individuals and yet they are physically, emotionally, intellectually, and spiritually related to each other. There is something in the man that cries out for the woman and something within the woman that longs for the companionship of the man. To deny our similarities is to deny our basic humanity. To deny our differences is a futile effort to refute reality. In a healthy marriage, our theme is never competition but rather cooperation. We find in each other a resting place, a home, a relative, one to whom we are deeply and uniquely related.

Sexual intimacy is one aspect of unity. However, the emotional, intellectual, and spiritual areas of life cannot be separated from the physical. This was the mistake of the couple sitting in my office—he wanted sexual intimacy; she pleaded for emotional closeness, but neither recognized that they were asking for the same thing. They wanted to feel close to each other, to feel accepted, to feel loved. Their focus was on different aspects of the same reality.

In a healthy marriage, the couple has come to understand that their desire for intimacy is a part of who they are. It is one of the reasons they married in the first place. Most couples can look back on a period in their relationship when they talked of being "in love." They experienced a deep sense of closeness. It all began with a physical, emotional attraction for each other that I call "the tingles." It is the tingles that motivate us to date. The whole purpose of the dating phenomenon is to "get to know each other," which is simply another phrase for intimacy. When the "in-love stage" is fully developed, we have a sense of belonging to each other. We feel that somehow we were meant for each other. We experience the willingness to be open and honest, to tell our deepest secrets. We sense in our hearts that we will love each other forever, that we want each other's happiness above all else, and that our own happiness is dependent upon being with this person forever. It is this deep sense of intimacy that gives us the courage to make a lifetime commitment to marriage. (The in-love experience is discussed more fully in my book *The Five Love Languages*, chapter 1.[2])

A WALL OF DISAPPOINTMENTS

Jennifer was crying as I handed her the box of tissues from my credenza. "I just don't understand it," she said. "Before marriage, I felt so close to Rob. We shared everything. He was so kind and tender and understanding. He wrote me poems and gave me flowers, but now all of that is gone. I just don't know him anymore. He is not the man I married. We can't even talk without getting into an argument. We seem so far apart. I know he must be as miserable as I am. I know he is not happy."

What has happened to the intimacy between Jennifer and Rob? The answer is as old as creation itself. Genesis describes the beginnings of the relationship between the first woman and the first man: "Adam and his wife were both naked, and they felt no shame."[3] Male and female naked without shame. It is a graphic picture of marital intimacy. Two distinct persons equal in value with bone-deep emotional, spiritual, and physical relatedness; totally transparent without fear of being known. It is that kind of openness, acceptance, trust, and excitement to which every married couple aspires.

But a few pages later we read that the same man and woman sewed fig leaves together and made coverings for themselves after they had disobeyed God. They hid themselves from God and from each other. Now there was reason for shame. There was the experience of fear, and no longer could the man and woman tolerate nakedness. The guilt was too intense; the shame was unbearable. Intimacy was marred. The first thing Adam did was to blame Eve, and she in turn blamed the serpent. Before the day was over, God had announced the results of their sin, made them garments of animal skins for covering, and directed them out of the beautiful garden. Paradise is now only a memory, and pain is a reality.

Most couples only dream of the perfect intimacy of Paradise. We may start married life with a relatively high measure of intimacy, but at some point we replace intimacy with isolation.

How does this loss of intimacy occur? Many couples have described it as a wall developing between them. Let me suggest that a wall is always built one block at a time. Perhaps you can remember an episode like the following in the early weeks of your marriage. Matt and Emily had been married for only a month. Everything was going along fine until Thursday evening when Matt got off the phone and said excitedly to Emily, "Guess what? That was Dave. We're going down to the game on Saturday."

"Excuse me? I thought we'd agreed we were going to work around the house this weekend. You were going to help me with some stuff," Emily said.

"But—"

"You're married. Remember? Dave's not. He doesn't care. Matt, you can't just pick up and go with the guys anymore."

This experience was like putting a block in a wall between the two of them. But in those days, they were still "in love," so they got over the hurt, the disappointment. In a few days, things were pretty much back to normal. They got over it, but the block was still there. Two months later, there was another experience and another block, and then another and another. Before long, a wall was erected that Matt and Emily never intended to build. The intimacy was gone, and they were separated by a wall of disappointments.

How can a couple regain intimacy? The answer is simple but not easy: the wall must be torn down. One must go to the other and say, "I've been thinking about us, and I have realized that the problem isn't just with you. I've been looking back at our marriage and thinking about the times that I have failed you. I remember quite a few. I would like to remind you of these, and I would like to ask you to forgive me."

The moment you are willing to admit your failures and ask forgiveness, the wall on your side comes tumbling down. If your spouse chooses to forgive you and in turn acknowledges his or her failures, the wall is torn down on both sides, and intimacy returns almost immediately. In order to keep the wall torn down, we must practice acknowledging our failures as quickly as possible after they occur. None of us is perfect. From time to time, we will disappoint our spouse, but if we are willing to acknowledge our failures and ask forgiveness, we can keep the walls torn down.

SPEAKING, LISTENING, UNDERSTANDING

Once those walls come down, we still have to work at building intimacy. We don't "obtain intimacy" and keep it as a treasure for the rest of our lives. Intimacy is fluid, not static, and it comes from open, honest, ongoing communication. Communication involves two simple elements: self-revelation, in which one is telling the other something of his or her thoughts, feelings, and experiences while the other is receiving this self-revelation as information and seeking to understand what the first person is thinking and feeling. The second in turn reveals his or her own thoughts, feelings, and experiences while the other listens and seeks to understand. The simple process of talking and listening maintains intimacy.

We are not mind readers. We can observe the behavior of our spouses, but we do not know what thoughts and feelings and motives lie behind the behavior. We can observe the other crying, but we do not know what produced the tears. We can see the other's angry behavior, but we do not innately know what gave rise to the furor. It is only as we reveal ourselves to each other that we can continue to have feelings of intimacy with each other. Why is this simple human skill of talking and listening so difficult in the context of marriage? We seemed to be experts in communication while we were dating. We spent hours talking and listening, revealing the inner secrets of our past and expressing our feelings in an open and sometimes even poetic way. Why does this ability to communicate become so difficult after marriage? In addition to the blocks we allow to divide us, there are other reasons that we fail to communicate on an intimate emotional level.

BURYING OUR EMOTIONS

Most couples will continue to talk on the level of nuts-and-bolts logistics long after emotional intimacy is gone. What time shall I pick up the children? When does the meeting begin? Are we going to eat out or at home tonight? What time is the furnace guy coming? Did you pay the Visa bill? I'm going to walk the dog. This level of discussing factual information can and often does continue a long time after emotional, intellectual, spiritual, and sexual intimacy have ended. But intimacy is not fostered by such superficial talk. Intimacy has its roots in sharing our passions, emotions, thoughts, experiences, desires, and frustrations. What hinders the free flow of communication on this deeper emotional level? Let me suggest some common hindrances.

One reason we do not discuss our feelings is that we are not in touch with them. For whatever reason, some of us have been trained to deny our emotions. Perhaps earlier in life someone led us to believe that our emotions were not acceptable. We never saw our father show sadness or weakness, only stoic silence. Our mother said, "Always look on the bright side." A grandmother said, "Big boys don't cry." Fear, negativism, sharing of what we really thought or wondered about—these things were discouraged growing up.

For others, the deep emotional pain experienced in childhood has colored their adult reality. The pain of parents' separation, the memory of physical or sexual abuse, the grief over the untimely death of a parent—these and other experiences of emotional pain were never processed as a child. The feelings lie deeply buried within the person. Years ago, the person stopped feeling because the pain was so intense. He separated his intellectual life from his emotional life and is no longer in touch with how he feels. When you ask this person, "How do you feel about your sister's cancer?" his response will be, "I don't have any feelings. I just hope she gets well." He is not evading the question. He simply is not in touch with the emotional side of his humanity. For this person to find health and healing, he will likely require the help of a trained counselor. It does not help for the spouse to condemn him for not discussing his emotions.

The second reason we are reluctant to discuss our emotions is that we fear our spouse's response. We may fear that he or she will condemn our feelings, tell us we shouldn't feel that way, become angry with us, or reject us. The reason for our fear may be rooted in experiences we have had with our spouse, or it may be rooted in our experience in childhood. Such fear serves as a substantial roadblock to emotional intimacy. To overcome such fears, we must first acknowledge them and ask for an opportunity to admit them. Only as we face these fears openly are we able to work through them and go beyond them.

Another reason some individuals do not talk more about emotions is that they have never done it in the past. "We have a good marriage, but we have never talked much about our feelings. Why should we start now?" Normally, the person who makes such a statement has come from a family where emotions were not admitted openly. The message was clear that around here, you don't talk about your feelings, especially if you think others will find them objectionable. So the person managed to live without opening his emotions. Thus, his or her entire marriage has been structured with little openness in the emotional area. The thought of doing something different is a bit frightening. But the discussing of emotions is a necessary way to build deeper intimacy in a relationship. And yes, emotional intimacy does affect sexual intimacy. We can never successfully separate the two.

There is one additional reason some do not discuss their emotions with their spouses: "I don't want to burden my spouse with my emotional struggles." Such a statement sounds caring on the surface, and the person may indeed be looking out for the interests of his or her spouse. There are times in which our spouses may be under so much stress that it may not be wise for us to discuss our emotions, especially if our emotions are negative. We may need to be listening to them as they talk about their emotions so that we can give them emotional support instead of further burdening them with our own problems. But in a healthy relationship, the discussion of emotions needs to be a two-way street. If we do not tell our negative feelings of hurt and disappointment, how can the other ever give us emotional support? We are denying our spouse the opportunity to be intimate with us and to enter into our struggles.

This sharing of the inner self is the fabric from which we weave marital intimacy. It is what we thought we had when we married. It is what we wanted to have for a lifetime. Without it, the whole relationship seems to wane. It is extremely important to a loving family. It satisfies the inner longings of the couple, and, if children are in the family, it serves as the best positive model of what family is all about.

Because the desire for marital intimacy is so deeply rooted in our psyche, it greatly affects all other aspects of family life. First, it affects the way the husband and wife treat each other. Then it influences the way they both relate to the children. When intimacy exists between a husband and wife, the results will be a healthy environment that is conducive to raising children. Where it does not exist, children will grow up in a battle zone and may wear the scars for a lifetime.

Time and effort spent in developing intimacy in your marriage is time wisely invested for the emotional and physical health of your children. In fact, few things will yield greater results for your children. Intimacy between the husband and the wife builds security in the life of the child. There is something deep within the child that says, "This is the way it is supposed to be."

CHAPTER FOUR

Five Steps to Intimacy

We did not marry in order to find a convenient way to cook meals, wash dishes, do laundry, run errands, and rear children. We married out of a deep desire to know and to be known by another, to love and to be loved, to live life together, believing that together we could experience life more deeply than apart.

How does this lofty and sometimes ethereal goal become something we can live out day to day? It helps to look at the five essential components of an intimate relationship.

Number 1: We share our thoughts (intellectual intimacy).

Number 2: We discuss our feelings (emotional intimacy).

Number 3: We spend time together and discuss the time we have spent apart (social intimacy).

Number 4: We open our souls to each other (spiritual intimacy).

Number 5: We share our bodies (physical intimacy).

In the living of life, these can never be segmented into five distinct boxes, but for purposes of learning, we will look at them separately.

"WHAT DO YOU THINK?":
UNDERSTANDING INTELLECTUAL INTIMACY

When we are awake, we live in the world of the mind. We are constantly thinking and making decisions based on those thoughts.

From the moment we arise, the mind is active. It takes the sights, sounds, and smells that we encounter through the senses and attaches meaning to them. With the first soft buzz of the alarm clock, the mind encourages us to get up (or to snooze another five minutes). We look in the refrigerator and see the milk is gone and decide whether to eat our cereal in water or to grab a donut on the way to the office. We think, we interpret, we decide—all in the realm of the mind. No one else knows what is going on inside our head. This goes on all day long (no wonder we sometimes get headaches!). In addition to processing what we experience through the five senses, the mind also has the capacity to roam. While doing one project, particularly if it is a routine project, the mind can visit the Grand Canyon, Pikes Peak, Lombard Street, or Beacon Hill. In the mind, we can traverse continents in milliseconds. We can see faces and hear voices that exist only in our memory.

The mind is also filled with desires. Desire motivates us to walk to the coffee machine or to go online and book a trip across the country. A desire is based on the idea that in the attaining of something or the doing of something, I will find pleasure or I will accomplish something of value. These ideas, called desires, motivate much of human behavior. Thus, the mind operates—all day, every day—filled with thoughts. The same is true for your spouse. You each live within your minds. Whether you are in the same room or miles apart, your mind is active with thoughts.

If we are to obtain intimacy, we must choose to reveal some of these thoughts to each other. Obviously we must be selective. The possibility of discussing all thoughts is absurd. Life is not that long! On the other hand, the choice to tell the other no thoughts assures the death of intimacy. So much of our lives are lived in the world of the mind that if we make time to tell some of our thoughts, our interpretations of the events in our lives that day, and the desires with which we have lived, we will experience intellectual intimacy.

When I speak of intellectual intimacy, I am not talking about discussing highly technical or so-called intellectual thoughts. The important thing is discussing *your* thoughts. They may be thoughts focused on finances, politics, food, race, health, or crime, but they are your thoughts. They reveal something of what has gone on in your mind throughout the day. When two minds link, there is the building of intellectual intimacy. Those minds do not contain the same thoughts or perspectives on what has been experienced—and that is the genius of intellectual intimacy. We have the high pleasure of learning something of the inner movements of our spouse's mind. That is the essence of intellectual intimacy.

ALLOWING ANOTHER INTO YOUR WORLD: UNDERSTANDING EMOTIONAL INTIMACY

Feelings are our spontaneous, emotional responses to what we encounter through the five senses. I hear that a friend's child is ill and I feel sad. I see the fire truck racing down the road and I feel troubled. You touch my hand and I feel loved. I see your smile and I feel encouraged.

All day long, every day, life is filled with feelings. You put your dollar in the drink machine and receive no drink (and no change). You have feelings! You are informed that the company for which you work is going to downsize. You have feelings! Your spouse calls and tells you she got a promotion at work. Your middle schooler argues with you. Your inner life is filled with feelings, but no one sees them. They may see certain behavior that is motivated by your feelings, but they cannot see your feelings. They see you laughing, but they do not know why. They see the furrowed brow, but they have, at best, only a partial idea what motivated it.

It is the *discussing* of emotions that builds emotional intimacy. Allowing another person into your inner world of feelings: being willing to say "I'm feeling a lot of fear right now" or "I am really happy tonight." "I was so encouraged when I heard . . ." "I really felt embarrassed last night about . . ." "The best way I know how to describe my feeling is to say that I feel hurt." These are statements of self-revelation. In making such statements, we are choosing to be intimate with our spouses, to reveal to them something of what is going on in our emotional world.

Learning to talk about emotions can be one of the most rewarding experiences of life. Such discussion requires an atmosphere of acceptance. If I am assured that my spouse will not condemn my feelings or try to refute or change my feelings, I am far more likely to talk about them. If a wife says, "I've really been feeling depressed the last couple of days" and her husband's response is "Why should you feel depressed? With life as easy as you have it, how could you be depressed?" she will find it difficult to explain her feelings to him the next time. However, if he accepts her emotions and says, "I'm sorry to hear that. Why don't you tell me about it?" and listens attentively as she talks further about her feelings, he will create a climate where she will discuss them openly with him. This sense of security, where we know our spouse will receive what we are saying and not condemn or shame us for feeling that way, makes it easy to discuss feelings with each other.

The discussion of positive feelings allows us to enter into each other's joys. A wife eagerly tells her husband, "I am so excited. I just got an email from my best friend in high school! I have not heard from her in years." If the husband responds to his wife's excitement by saying, "That sounds exciting. What did she have to say?" and he listens as the wife continues to lay out her excitement over this word from the past, they will experience an emotionally intimate moment.

In the same manner, if we talk about negative feelings, we also create emotional intimacy. A wife says, "I am afraid that we are not going to have enough money to pay for Julie's college tuition next semester. I really feel bad about it, but I don't know what to do." The husband can answer such openness with a statement such as "I can see how that could be a very painful thought for you. Would you like to talk about what we might be able to do?" What follows will likely be further discussion of the financial situation, and perhaps together they will come up with an idea as to how they may accomplish this financial goal. In so doing, they have built emotional intimacy.

Discussing feelings—the highs and the lows—is one of the most satisfying aspects of marriage. When we tell our spouse about our emotions, we are including our spouse in a very powerful part of our lives. Shared positive emotions always intensify the pleasure, and shared negative emotions should always bring relief and support. In an intimate relationship, emotions are not seen as enemies, but as friends, and the discussion of emotions is a part of the normal flow of life.

SHARING EXPERIENCES:
UNDERSTANDING SOCIAL INTIMACY

Social intimacy has to do with spending time together around the events of life. Many of these events involve other people. Some of them we experience together; others happen while we are apart and are shared through open communication. Both build social intimacy. Much of life centers around encounters that happen throughout the day—things people say to us or do for us or with us or against us, situations that arise with which we are forced to deal. Our supervisor delivers us an encouraging word or drops a bombshell; Tim gets a D in algebra or Hannah comes home sick from school. Life is made up of a combination of routine and unexpected events. Many of these encounters take place while we are apart from our spouse. It is in verbally telling these events that we come to feel that we are a part of each other's experiences. Life is not limited to what happens to me throughout the day. As I talk with my spouse, our horizon is broadened. We feel that we are a part of what each other is doing.

We sense that we are a social unit, and each of us understands that what happens in the other's life is important.

This telling of events will often involve the discussion of thoughts and feelings. We tell each other how we interpret the events of life, and we may also explain the feelings that accompany these events. For many years in my marriage seminars, I have encouraged people to establish the practice of a "daily sharing time" in which each of them tells the other a minimum of "three things that happened in my life today and how I feel about them." In establishing this daily practice, many couples have indicated that the daily talking time has become the highlight of their day and that, in this time, they genuinely experience social intimacy.

There is another aspect of social intimacy, however, which involves the two of us *doing* events together. These times may be done in the presence of other people, such as going to a movie or attending an athletic event. Social activities are not limited to spectator events. We may go bowling together or play Scrabble or plant a dogwood tree in the front yard. We may even go shopping together (which would also be an act of service for some husbands). A picnic in the park or even on the deck can add excitement to an otherwise cloudy day. Much of life involves doing. When we do things together, we are not only developing a sense of teamwork, but we are also enhancing our sense of intimacy.

The things we do together often form our most vivid memories. Will we ever forget climbing Mount Mitchell together? Or who can forget giving the dog a bath? I held while you scrubbed. Then there were those times we went sledding together before the children came. Then with the children. And that one time at midnight when we slipped out and left the children in bed and had our own slide down toboggan hill.

In a loving family, social intimacy is a way of life. Time pressures, stresses, and other barriers must be negotiated, but there is conscious effort on the part of both husband and wife to continue to make time to experience life together, doing things that one or both of them enjoy.

ONE COUPLE, UNDER GOD:
UNDERSTANDING SPIRITUAL INTIMACY

Spiritual intimacy is often the least excavated of all the foundations of marital intimacy, yet it has a significant impact upon the other four areas of intimacy. As I began my anthropological studies many years ago, I was fascinated to discover that wherever we find man, we find a belief in the spirit world. Few aspects of human culture are "panhuman"—that is, found in all cultures. The belief in a spirit world is one of those panhuman realities. My own conclusion after years of study is that postmodern man's attempt to ignore or deny the reality of humankind's spiritual nature is a futile one. The current interest in Western culture in various forms of spirituality is evidence that postmodern Western man is still in search of a soul.

My own personal conviction is that when modern man left the ancient Christian faith in search of enlightenment through scientific materialism, he left the fountain of spiritual truth. I have been drinking from that fountain for many years and find it the source of great tranquility.

Since marriage involves two individuals seeking to build intimacy, their individual perceptions and experiences in the spiritual realm are something to be discussed. The notion that religion is "personal" and something about which one does not talk is the same misconception that emotions are personal and not something to be discussed. When we categorically refuse for whatever reason to discuss our spiritual perceptions, we are eliminating an entire aspect of our humanity, and thus we limit marital intimacy.

Spiritual intimacy does not require agreement of belief on every detail. As in all other areas of intimacy, we are seeking to tell each other what is going on in the inner self. When we talk about our emotions, thoughts, and experiences, we are telling something the other person would not have known unless we had chosen to talk about it. The process is much the same in building spiritual intimacy. We are each telling the other our own personal thoughts, experiences, feelings, and interpretations of spiritual things. The purpose is not agreement but understanding. Obviously if we hold the same core beliefs, then our level of intellectual agreement will be high, but even then our experiences, our emotions, and our interpretations of spiritual things will not always be identical. For example, you may have spent a great deal of time this week reflecting upon the love of God—while I have been reading about the wrath of God. I am trying to understand and process one aspect of God's nature while you are meditating and reflecting upon another aspect. If we are willing to open this part of our lives to each other, we can both be richer, and spiritual intimacy is the result.

Some time ago my wife entered my office with enthusiasm and said, "I must read this to you." She proceeded to read a rather lengthy portion of "The Purchase of a Soul," taken from *Les Misérables* by Victor Hugo.[1] She read the portion where the Bishop of Digne was interacting with a man who had been a convict for nineteen years and was only recently released. The man was overcome with the idea that the bishop would have him in his home for a meal since he had been refused both lodging and food at several establishments in the village. "You don't even know my name," the man said, to which the bishop responded, "Oh, but I do know your name. 'Your name is my brother.'" She went on to read the loving way in which the bishop responded to this man who had lived such a difficult life. She then told me her own feelings and thoughts with regard to this passage and reminded me of the time she saw *Les Misérables* in New York. In her talking and in my listening, we experienced a moment of spiritual intimacy.

Spiritual intimacy is discussing with each other some of your thoughts about spiritual realities. Tricia read Psalm 23 yesterday morning and was captivated by the personal pronouns, "The LORD is my shepherd; I shall not want. He maketh me to lie down in green pastures . . ." (KJV). Last night she discussed this with Art, and he told her about his experience with a shepherd in Australia before they were married. They experienced spiritual intimacy.

Spiritual intimacy is fostered not only by verbal communication, but also by shared experience. Jim and Judy have attended Sunday morning worship services together regularly. "There is something about experiencing the service together that gives me a sense of closeness to Jim. We share the same hymnbook; I hear him sing the same words I am singing. We hold hands during the prayers and listen and take notes from the pastor's sermon. Usually on the way home, we tell each other one thing that we liked about the service that morning."

Praying together is another way of building spiritual intimacy. Few things are more personal than sincere prayer. Two people joining in honest prayer will discover a deep sense of spiritual unity. We are seldom more vulnerable than when we are praying sincere prayers with each other. For those who find it uncomfortable to say verbal prayers in the presence of their spouse, I suggest silent praying. Hold hands, close your eyes, and pray silently. When you finish, say "Amen" aloud. When the other person says "Amen," you will know he or she has finished praying. No words are uttered audibly, but your hearts move closer to each other. You have experienced a moment of spiritual intimacy.

"ONE FLESH":
UNDERSTANDING PHYSICAL INTIMACY

Because men and women are sexually different (long live the difference!), we often come to sexual intimacy in different ways. The husband's emphasis is most often on the physical aspects of sexual intimacy. The seeing, the touching, the feeling, the experience of foreplay and climax are the focus of his attention. It is physically exciting, exhilarating, and satisfying, and many would say it is the greatest physical pleasure in life. The wife, on the other hand, most often comes to sexual intimacy with an emphasis on the emotional aspect. To feel loved, cared for, admired, appreciated, and treated tenderly brings her great joy. If the sexual encounter is preceded by words of affirmation and acts of love—if, in short, she feels truly loved—then the sexual experience is but an extension of this emotional pleasure. She will enjoy the physical orgasm, but she does not live for that moment. Her pleasure is derived far more from the emotional closeness that she feels to her husband in the sexual experience.

Sexual intimacy requires understanding and responding to these differences. The husband must learn to focus on his wife's emotional need for love, and she must understand the physical aspect of his sexuality. If the couple focuses on making the sexual experience an act of love for each other and will take the time to learn how to give pleasure to each other, they will find sexual intimacy. But if they simply "do what comes naturally," they will find sexual frustration.

There are also differences in the area of sexual arousal. Men are stimulated by sight. Simply watching his wife undress in the shadows of the bedroom light may give him an erection. (I'm sorry, men. They can watch us undress and be unmoved. I mean, the thought never even crosses their minds.) Women are far more stimulated sexually by tender touch, affirming words, and acts of thoughtfulness. That is why many wives have said, "Sex doesn't begin in the bedroom. It begins in the kitchen. It doesn't start at night, it starts in the morning." The way she is treated and spoken to throughout the day will have a profound effect upon her sexual arousal.

Thus, it should be obvious that we cannot separate sexual intimacy from emotional, intellectual, social, and spiritual intimacy. We have looked at these separately for the purpose of understanding, but in the context of human relationships, they can never be compartmentalized. We cannot attain sexual intimacy without intimacy in the other areas of life. We can have sex but not sexual intimacy—the sense of closeness, of being one, of finding mutual satisfaction.

The Bible says that when a husband and wife have sexual intercourse, they become "one flesh." The idea is not that they lose their identity, but that in the act of intercourse, their two lives are bonded together in a mutually satisfying way. It is not simply a way of joining two bodies that were uniquely made for each other, but it speaks of intellectual, emotional, social, and spiritual bonding as well. It is the physical expression of the inward union of two lives. In the ancient Hebrew writings and the first-century Greek writings of the early church, sexual intercourse was always reserved for marriage. It was not an arbitrary denunciation of sexual intercourse outside of marriage; it was simply an effort to be true to the nature of sexual intercourse. Such deep bonding would be inappropriate outside a loving, lifelong commitment between a husband and a wife.

In a healthy family, the relationship between the husband and the wife is, without question, the most significant relationship. In this relationship, nothing is more important than marital intimacy. Sexual intimacy is the most physical expression of this intimacy. And the success of sexual intimacy is greatly affected by intellectual, emotional, social, and spiritual intimacy.

MARITAL INTIMACY AND FAMILY SECURITY

Stress, times of separation, sickness, work, children, and other normal cares of life will affect the time and energy invested in marital intimacy, but in a loving family, the husband and wife are committed to keeping intimacy alive. Such an intimate relationship not only brings deep satisfaction to the couple but also serves as a model to the children in the family. It is this model that is so desperately lacking in many contemporary families.

What about our live-in anthropologist? What did John see of marital intimacy in our relationship? Well, of course we did not invite John into the bedroom, but he did sometimes catch us kissing on the couch. In his own words . . .

> Karolyn was more demonstrative; she is a hugger. I considered you to be more reserved, but it was clear that you loved each other dearly. There was real security. I can remember you reaching out and putting your arm around her, touching her arm, being very affectionate in that way. I always enjoyed hearing how you two got together and how Karolyn had at first resisted. She was honest about that time in her life; she really came around and loved you passionately and with her whole heart, and you the same for her. I always sensed a great respect on both your parts—it was obvious that you tremendously respected her and listened to her, let her speak and did not interrupt her, and you would do the same for me too. I also thought you were transparent. You were very honest about having worked through difficult times in your earlier years. I found this extremely encouraging.

On occasion, John volunteered to babysit so that Karolyn and I could attend social functions. (We tried not to take advantage of John as a convenient babysitter; we knew that was not the main purpose of his presence.) Other times we took the children with us as we walked to a nearby park, and while keeping a watchful eye on the children, Karolyn and I discussed thoughts, feelings, and experiences from our day. It was our pattern to have the children to bed by 8:30. This allowed "couple time" for the two of us.

We worked hard to be together for the evening meal. This was our time for reporting to each other what had happened through the day. John was an integral part of this discussion. After John was gone and the children moved into the teenage years, we continued this tradition, although it meant with basketball practice and other extracurricular school activities that our dinner meal bounced from 4:00 p.m. until 9:00 p.m. For us, it was a commitment; it was family at its best, coming together intellectually, emotionally, and socially. Now that the children are grown, when they return for occasional visits, the dinner table is the focus of our "together time." We can sit for hours and catch up on our time apart.

Intimacy between the husband and wife spills over into the rest of family relationships. If intimacy is missing in the marital relationship, it will likely be distorted in parent-child relationships and in sibling relationships. In healthy families, husbands and wives make the marriage top priority, realizing that intimacy between a husband and wife not only serves their own needs but provides the highest level of emotional security for children. I am fully convinced that my greatest contribution to the children of this generation lies in helping their mothers and fathers build intimate marriages.

We have always told our children about our personal struggle in building marital intimacy. I was convinced that our son, Derek, understood that struggle and the sweet fruit of intimacy when he gave me the poem that follows.

Tonight, a train passes through
the valley below our home.
A long whistle sounds, gathering all
the unheard nights into its calling.

My parents, deep asleep
and me, listen through
the window.

They, too, gathering so many long nights—
Nights before my birth
Nights in the Texas desert
trying to force a forfeit from one another;
Nights of waiting for the other
to come to bed after a day
of unspoken argumentation,
Nights of wondering if this
was meant to be after all.

And after all those long ago nights
the word home finally formed
on its own.
And breakfast comes with cheer
to the children, and dishes are cleared
and dried without complaint;
And we children wonder
at what seems like daily sacrifice
but comes to us
Like a train being passed through
a long valley, unheard
and now sounding this
intimate whistle of wisdom.

For more information on how you and your spouse can build intimacy, see the code on page 177 to access the Family Adventure Guide at **www.5lovelanguages.com/5traits**. This guide is to help put into practice the healthy traits discussed in this book. You'll find a number of assessments, things to think about, and opportunities for deeper discussion.

PART THREE

Parents Who Guide

CHAPTER FIVE

Talking, Doing, Loving

In a healthy family, parents take the responsibility to guide their children—to teach, to train, and, yes, to discipline. In the ancient Greek world, two words described the function of parents: *teaching* and *training*. The Greek word for teaching, *nouthesia*, literally means "a putting into the mind." In the Greek way of thinking, this was done by verbal admonition; thus, teaching by words. The word for training is *paideia*. It is sometimes translated "nurture," at other times "chastening." To the Greeks, training always involved action. It had both a positive and negative aspect. The nurturing aspect may have involved hugging and kissing a child, whereas the chastening aspect may have involved physically restraining him from danger, but the emphasis in both was upon taking action.

Knowing when to apply these various means of guidance is not always easy—as any parent can attest. Some parents have vowed they will always explain everything to their children, never declaring, "Because I said so." The main theme of their parenting style is "Let's talk about this." For some, "talking" means a monologue in which they give the child another lecture, whereas others emphasize the importance of dialogue, making sure they hear the child's thoughts as well as expressing their own. But for both, the emphasis is on teaching by word. They are big on reason; they want to answer the "why" questions for children. They operate on the philosophy that if children understand *why*, they are far more likely to respond positively to the parent's rule or request. Some of these parents who emphasize words to the exclusion of actions are reacting to physically abusive patterns of discipline from their own parents. They have vowed to themselves that they will never treat their children the way they were treated.

The negative side to the "words only" approach to childrearing is that when the children do not respond to calm words and reason, parents often end up yelling, screaming, and verbally threatening their children to bring them into line. Over time, little Ella and Evan learn the same pattern of response, and the home becomes a battleground of words. The one in control is the one who screams the loudest and longest.

Another group of parents emphasizes action to the exclusion of words. Their theme is "Act now, talk later." For many of them, later never comes. When the child is misbehaving, they immediately yank him up by the shoulder straps, give him a few strong whacks, put him back in the grocery cart, and expect him not to cry. Their parenting motto is "Actions speak louder than words." The child must be put in his place. If you don't give strong discipline, he will get out of hand. These are the parents who often end up physically abusing children. Because the child does not respond positively to their earlier actions, they use more stringent actions and end up doing things they never dreamed they would do.

In a healthy family, parents balance words and actions. They take time to explain the rules and the consequences of breaking rules. They also take loving action when they administer the consequences. When this balance is attained, parents are less likely to go to the extremes of yelling, screaming, and threatening on the one side or physical abuse on the other side. They are far more likely to attain their objective of helping the child develop into an emotionally healthy adult.

LOVING COMES FIRST

By now some of you are asking, "Is it really possible for two parents who have very different approaches to childrearing to find a meeting of the minds?" The answer is an unqualified yes. In our own family, we discovered that I tended to be a quiet, calm, "let's talk about it" parent, while Karolyn tended to be an impulsive, "take action now" kind of person. It took us a while to realize what was happening, analyze our patterns, and admit to each other our basic tendencies. When this was done and we began to concentrate on the question "What is best for our children?" we found that we could work together as a team and that, in fact, we must. Our basic tendencies did not change, but we did learn to temper those tendencies. I learned how to take responsible action and to blend words and actions. Karolyn learned to think before she moved. In the following chapters, I will tell some of the ideas that helped us in the process. But first, let's take a look at the first and most important element parents need to guide their children.

No pattern of guidance and discipline will be highly effective if the child does not feel loved by the parents. Conversely, if the child feels loved, even poor attempts at teaching and training may still produce a healthy adult.

I once read the story of an ordinary man: one wife, two sons, comfortable house, meaningful vocation. All went well until one night one of the sons became ill. Believing the illness to be nothing serious, the parents gave the child an aspirin and went to bed. The child died during the night of acute appendicitis. The grief and guilt of that experience drove the man to alcohol. In time, his frustrated wife left him. He was now a single parent with one son, Ernie, and an alcohol problem.

With the passing of time, his alcoholism led to the loss of his job and eventually the loss of his house, possessions, and self-respect.

Eventually he died in a motel room, alone. But the son turned out to be a well-adjusted, hardworking, generous adult. Knowing the circumstances of his rearing, somebody asked the son, "I know that you and your father lived alone for many years. I know something of his problem with alcohol. What did he do that caused you to turn out to be such a loving, kind, and generous person?"

Upon reflection the young man said, "As long as I can remember from the time I was a child until I was eighteen years of age, every night my father would come into my bedroom, kiss me on the cheek, and say, 'I love you, Son.'"[1] Love does cover a multitude of sins.

Apparently the love Ernie felt from his father's words of affirmation and physical touch filled his emotional love tank and gave him the ability to develop a positive outlook on life in spite of his father's other failures. Unfortunately, words of affirmation and a kiss will not make all children feel loved. My book *The Five Love Languages of Children* emphasizes the importance of discovering your child's primary love language and speaking it regularly.[2] I am convinced that there are five emotional love languages and that every child understands one of these languages more clearly than the others. Let me briefly review the five.

LOVE LANGUAGE #1: WORDS OF AFFIRMATION

Ernie's father was speaking two of the five primary languages of love—words of affirmation and physical touch. Let's examine the first of these. Giving a child positive words about himself and your assessment of him is one of love's basic languages. The following are all words of affirmation: "Good job!" "Thanks for your help." "I like the way you did that; I can tell you worked hard." "I appreciate it." "Great play." "Thanks for your help this afternoon." "You look really strong." "You are so beautiful." "I love you." These expressions of affirmation are important in communicating love to all children, but for the child whose primary love language is words of affirmation, they are his or her emotional lifeblood.

LOVE LANGUAGE #2: QUALITY TIME

Quality time involves giving the child your undivided attention. For the child whose primary love language is quality time, nothing will suffice but giving him extended periods of attention. This time may be spent reading books, playing ball, riding bikes, taking walks, or simply talking as you drive to the restaurant. These are the times that make the child feel loved. The words "I love you" apart from spending quality time with this child will seem like empty chatter. The parent's words may be sincere, but the child will not feel loved.

LOVE LANGUAGE #3: PHYSICAL TOUCH

We have long known the power of physical touch as a communicator of love. Research has shown that babies who are touched frequently in a loving way grow up with better emotional health than those who are left unattended. Touch is crucial to all children, but it is in receiving affectionate touching that some children feel most loved. The manner in which this touch is given will certainly have to be modified as the child gets older. Hugging a teenager in the presence of his friends may cause feelings of embarrassment rather than love. But if the teen's primary love language is physical touch, he craves the touching when the friends are not around.

LOVE LANGUAGE #4: RECEIVING GIFTS

Giving and receiving gifts is a universal expression of love. A gift says "Dad/Mom was thinking about me." When you return from a trip and bring a child a gift, it says that he was in your thoughts while you were away. This does not mean that you must give the child with this primary love language everything he requests in order for the child to feel loved. It does mean that there must be a significant number of gifts given or the child will not feel loved. The gifts need not be expensive. It is truly "the thought that counts."

LOVE LANGUAGE #5: ACTS OF SERVICE

Doing things for the child that you know the child appreciates is another of love's basic languages. Preparing meals, washing clothes, providing transportation, helping with homework, and attending a child's sporting event are all expressions of love. To the child whose primary language of love is acts of service, such acts become essential to the child's emotional well-being. Fixing the bicycle means more than getting the child back on wheels; it is applying the oil of love.

I like psychiatrist and author Ross Campbell's "love tank" concept.[3] He believes that inside every child is an emotional love tank. When the child feels genuinely loved by the parents, the child will develop normally and be open to instruction and training. When the child's love tank is empty and the child does not feel loved by the parents, the child will likely rebel at the parents' efforts at guiding and disciplining.

All of these are valid expressions of love to a child, but they are not all of equal value to every child. Out of the five love languages, each child has a primary and secondary love language. These two are more important than the other three. If a parent consistently speaks the primary love language and the secondary love language of a child, the child will feel loved. If the parents do not speak these consistently and regularly, the child may feel unloved although the parents are expressing love in any of the other three languages. It is not enough that the parent loves the child. The question is, "Does the child feel loved?" Every counselor has encountered children, young and old, who say, "My parents don't love me. They love my brother, but they don't love me." In almost every case the parents love the child very deeply; the problem is they have not spoken the primary love language of the child. Thus, the child has grown up with an empty love tank.

DISCOVERING YOUR CHILDREN'S LOVE LANGUAGES

How do you discover the primary love language of your children? Let me suggest three ways. First, observe how they express love to you. If your son regularly tells you what a good parent you are and what a good job you do preparing meals, and so forth, his love language is likely words of affirmation. If your daughter is always bringing you gifts she has made and wrapped in gift paper or gifts she has found in the yard, then her love language is likely receiving gifts. If a child is always wanting to hug and touch you, suspect that the number one love language is physical touch. If he continually wants to help you with your work around the house, then likely his love language is acts of service. If she constantly wants to play with you, read books with you, and do things with you, her love language is most likely quality time. Your children are giving to you what they like to receive themselves.

My son's love language is physical touch. I learned it when he was about four. When I came home in the afternoon he would run up to me, jump on my lap, and mess up my hair. He was touching me because he wanted to be touched. When he came home for a weekend as a young adult, he would lie on the floor watching television. When I walked through the room and he needed love, he would trip me. Physical touch still speaks loudly to him.

On the other hand, our daughter's love language is quality time. This motivated me to spend many evenings walking with my daughter when she was in high school, discussing books, boys, and other topics. She is now a physician, but when she comes home for a visit, she will say, "Want to take a walk, Dad?" Quality time still communicates love to her.

My son would never walk with me. He said, "Walking's dumb! You're not going anywhere. If you're going somewhere, drive." What makes one child feel loved will not necessarily make another feel loved. The key is to learn the primary love language of each child and speak that language consistently. Once you are speaking their primary and secondary love languages, you can sprinkle the other three in along the way. They will give added bonus points, but you dare not neglect the primary and secondary love languages of your children.[4]

After noticing what your children do for you, observe what your children request of you most often. Those requests will be a reflection of their primary love language. If your child says to you as you leave on a trip, "Be sure to bring me something," he is giving you a clear clue to his primary love language. If he regularly asks, "How did I do, Mommy?" he is telling you that words of affirmation is his primary language. If your son is continually requesting that you walk with him or play with him or do things with him, he is revealing that his primary language is quality time. Listen to your children's requests carefully until you see a pattern emerging. Once you see one of the five love languages standing out in their list of requests, assume that is their language and begin to focus on that as either the primary or secondary love language.

A third clue is to listen for what your children complain about most often. If they are critical of you because you don't play with them or you don't bring them gifts or you didn't mention the A they made on their report card, they are giving you a clue as to their primary love language. Children are most critical in the area of life that is related to their primary love language.

Until you are certain of your child's primary and secondary love languages, focus on a different one each month and see how your child responds during the month. When you are speaking the child's primary language, the child will tend to be more receptive to your teaching and training. He will tend to have a more positive spirit about life in general and will tend to promote family harmony. When his love tank is empty, the child will be at his or her worst.

CHAPTER SIX

The Challenge of Creative Teaching

What parent has not been driven to despair by the seemingly endless stream of *what* and *why* questions asked by the thirsty child? Children are naturally curious. What is sad is that some parents have killed this inquisitive spirit by "Not now" and "Because I said so" answers.

The challenge of the teaching parent is to learn to cooperate with the child's natural desire for knowledge and to do it in such a way as to keep the child's mind open to a lifetime of learning. That is why I use the term "creative teaching." It is the challenge of creating an atmosphere where the child's desire to learn and the parents' desire to teach flow in a normal rhythm, making the experience enjoyable for both. The joy of learning is a well of unending pleasure for the child who is taught creatively. It is this well of joy that the teaching parent seeks to tap.

As parents, we must accept the reality that teaching our children will consume a portion of our lives. Ideally, this teaching will be on a consistent, daily basis. One of the great barriers in the contemporary world to parental teaching is time. With the majority of parents working outside the home, with long commutes or the myriad other time pressures families face, the sheer pressure of time makes creative teaching difficult.

It is beyond the scope of this book to give specific answers to the time struggle. But it is my strong conviction that we must choose to make time to teach our children. In our society, we have roughly eighteen years to take children from total dependence to relative independence; eighteen years to instill in them the skills of learning that we believe will serve them for a lifetime, to share with them our knowledge and values in such a way that they can genuinely evaluate and choose their own interests and values. Ours is an awesome task, and it deserves our best efforts at making time to do a good job. Let's examine four basic areas of creative teaching.

"THIS IS IMPORTANT"

Perhaps the first thought that comes to your mind when you think of teaching is instructing. Instructing is using words to communicate to the child something the parent believes to be important. It involves conveying family history and traditions, social dos and don'ts, intellectual facts and theories, moral and spiritual values, and practical insights on all aspects of life that we believe will make the child's life more productive and meaningful. The father conveys to the daughter that in our culture, we drive on the right-hand side of the road, wear seat belts, and drive at the speed limit. In doing so, he assures her, she is far more likely to live to adulthood. Parents give information about sexuality and health, about friends and boundaries, about animals and plants, about attitudes and behaviors. It is what the anthropologists call the enculturation process. It is teaching a child how to live as a part of the culture. It involves teaching certain social skills, certain bodies of information upon which the child can build a successful life.

In our society, this process is not left to parents alone. The school, the church, and other social organizations all accept part of the responsibility for helping a child develop and discover his place in society. But in our highly organized and highly technological society, parents continue to maintain the fundamental responsibility for equipping children for growth and survival in the modern world.

When some of us think of instruction, we visualize a teacher standing in front of a classroom giving lectures on how to multiply, divide, or do fractions. But good teaching is never limited to monologue. It does include formal instruction, but it also includes informal conversation—dialogue. We are not simply pouring information into the heads of our children; we are relating to persons who have feelings, thoughts, and choices to make. Thus, the most effective way of teaching involves dialogue between parent and child. Sometimes the parent is taking the initiative: "I want to tell you something my mother told me." Other times, the child is taking the lead: "Why does the bear sleep all winter?" Both are valid approaches to teaching. Our challenge is to do both creatively. So, if the family saying passed down from Grandma can be put on a three-by-five card and given to the child along with the verbal discussion of the information, the child is far more likely to learn the value of her grandmother's statement. In fact, she may even post the three-by-five card on her mirror and read it until she has memorized it. Eventually she is likely to apply Grandma's wisdom to her own life.

PART OF ALL OF LIFE

In the normal flow of life, when do we find time to give creative instruction? It is hard to improve on the early Hebrew model that instructed parents to teach their children as they were sitting in the home, walking along the road, when they were preparing for bed, and when they got up each morning.[1] In other words, creative teaching is not limited to a "teaching period" during the day; it is a part of all of life. It is to be done anytime we are awake and together.

Having studied Jewish family life and being deeply impressed with the solidarity of the ancient Jewish family, Karolyn and I took this model of parental teaching seriously. Could we, in our contemporary culture, teach our children while we were sitting around the house, walking along the road, in the evening before bedtime, and in the morning? We discovered that these four paradigms for teaching fit well into the modern world, although they take consistent effort.

In the morning: Though Karolyn's preparation of breakfast for the family was a tremendous act of service on her part, this was not Karolyn's prime time for teaching the children (except by her example of loving service). So I took the responsibility of the teaching parent in the morning. Our time was brief; it was around the table, usually at the conclusion of the meal. I read a brief passage, discussed an idea, gave the children an opportunity to ask questions or make comments. Then we prayed a brief prayer.

This teaching time seldom took more than five minutes. I would not say that this was our best teaching time of the day, but it was a time where we all could connect for a moment with each other and with a wholesome idea. This allowed us to begin our day apart with an awareness that we had been together as family. If the sense of family is experienced in the morning, it serves as a reminder throughout the day that there is always a family to come home to. If all the content was forgotten, the sense of "family together" was enough to make this teaching time worthwhile.

Sitting around the house: Does the modern family ever "sit around the house"? Yes, we sit and watch TV or stare at computer or phone screens, but we seldom sit together as parent and child for the purpose of teaching. We sit, but we do not talk. That is not to say that the TV and the computer are not vehicles of instruction. They are instructing and often doing it creatively, but unless content is carefully selected, they may not be giving the instruction the parents would deem wise. Unless these modern tools of instruction are used by parents as a creative means of instruction, they may become the enemy rather than the friend of parental instruction.

Our family did sit around the house and talk, parents and children exchanging ideas, feelings, and experiences. Our primary time for sitting around the house was at the evening meal. It was not unusual for us to spend an hour after the meal in such dialogue. As the children got older, these discussions became longer. When they came home from college, these times of informal chatting were known to extend to as much as three hours. The friends who accompanied our children on these weekend home visits were astounded that a family could sit and talk for three hours. Many of them had grown up in families where they never sat around and talked.

As a young father, I was early impressed with a statement attributed to Dr. Graham Blaine, chief psychiatrist at Harvard University, who said that the most serious problem with television was not its poor programming but that it destroyed the average family's conversation at the evening meal.[2] When people are anxious to see a favorite program, they hurry through the meal. What happened during the day, the little things and the bigger matters, are never discussed. Karolyn and I were committed to maintaining the tradition of an evening meal together, and we chose to use this as a time for instruction.

It would not have been recognized as instruction by the children. It was a time for talking, a time for being family, a time for listening to the events and feelings and frustrations of each other's experience. There was time to develop the sense of family and to establish the reality that family is always interested in the events of the day, the thoughts of the mind, and the decisions for the future. I confess that when the kids were in their teenage years, it took marathon effort to sustain this tradition. The evening meal had to be moved on a continuum from 4:00 p.m. to 9:00 p.m., depending on basketball games, drama rehearsals, and piano lessons. But we found it worth the effort, and our now grown children remember it as the time we talked together.

Walking along the road: When Moses first suggested this paradigm for the Hebrew parents of his day, the primary mode of transportation was walking. Mankind has always been "on the move." Whether one's livelihood is made by hunting, fishing, and berry picking or going to New York to close a business deal, people travel. Only the mode of travel has changed. It is in the car that families move from home to school or church or the mall or the ball game. These are excellent times for dialogue between parents and children. It is not formal instruction, but it is powerful instruction. It is on these trips that children often raise the questions they are grappling with.

Sometimes they ask for information, but often they ask the "why" questions. This gives parents an excellent opportunity for discussing their values with the child. Parents who have not found satisfactory values for their own lives often become frustrated with their children's why questions and end up avoiding those questions as often as possible. On the other hand, parents who hold firm values and hold them very deeply are sometimes inclined to be dogmatic and domineering in trying to instill their values in their children. Values, however, are best passed on to the next generation not by dogmatism but by modeling and dialogue. Let your children observe your life, and they will see what is important to you. Let them ask questions and give them honest answers, and they will have the best opportunity of internalizing your values. Ultimately, the growing child may reject or accept parental values, but the healthy process is dialogue. Such dialogue most often occurs in the informal settings of life while we are on the way to do other things.

Before bedtime: In all cultures, men, women, and children sleep. And in many cultures, the time just before bedtime is seen as an excellent time for parental instruction. In my own anthropological journeys, I have observed Tzeltal Indians in southern Mexico and Carib Indians on the island of Dominica. I have seen mothers cuddle young children beside an open fire and sing lullabies—creative instruction at its best. I have seen fathers gather young children around the fire and tell stories of Carib and Tzeltal history, which caused young minds to sleep with feelings of security and to dream of distant years. The modern contemporary world, far removed from those tribal fires, provides the same opportunities for instruction.

Because children want to postpone bedtime, they are often eager for instruction in any form. Songs, prayers, and stories all provide avenues for instruction before bedtime. In our home, John observed the following bedtime ritual. Karolyn or I would sit with the two children on the couch, TV off (fireplace on in the winter), and read from one of a number of storybooks we had collected through the years. After the story, there were always questions—questions related to the story or questions that flashed in a young mind like lightning in the sky and could not wait to be asked. We had a set bedtime, but we were willing to extend it if it seemed to be a teachable moment.

Then followed the last visit to the bathroom and the last drink of water before sliding between the sheets. Once in bed, it was time for prayers. Bedtime was staggered, with Derek, the younger, going to bed first, and Shelley, the older, going to bed ten to fifteen minutes later. This allowed time for personal prayers with each child. They prayed for the dog, Zacchaeus; they prayed for their teachers at school; and they prayed for whatever else came into their creative minds. Shelley always prayed for Dr. Al Hood, missionary physician in Thailand. Now a physician herself, Shelley acknowledges that her interest and prayers for Dr. Hood molded her own desire to become a physician. Yes, bedtime rituals are important.

Anytime parents and children are together is a good time for instruction. Creative instruction involves using the informal times when parent and child are together to verbally discuss ideas, feelings, desires, memories, or anything else the parent deems important or in which the child expresses interest. It is the parent seeking to lead the child in the magic of dialogue.

CREATIVE ENCOURAGEMENT

The second area of creative teaching is creative encouragement. The word *encourage* means "to instill courage." Courage is that state of mind that gives the child the ability to explore possibilities, to take risks, to accomplish what others may find impossible. How parents teach children has a great deal to do with whether the children are encouraged or discouraged. In healthy families, parents give children many encouraging words.

As parents, we must not wait till the child accomplishes perfection before we give encouraging words. Some parents are fearful that if they encourage the child for what the parent considers to be mediocre work, the child will never rise above the level of the mediocrity. In reality, the opposite is true. If you refrain from encouraging the child's less-than-perfect efforts, the child will never rise to his or her potential.

We must learn to give children encouraging words for their efforts, not for the results. We do this rather naturally when children are young. Remember the first time your child tried to walk? He was standing by the couch, and you were two feet away saying to him, "That's right, you can do it. That's right; come on. Try. You can do it. That's right." The child took half a step and fell, and what did you say? You didn't say, "You dumb kid; can't you walk?" Rather, you clapped your hands wildly and said, "Yeah, yeah! That's right! That's right!" The child got up and tried again, and in due time, the child walked.

It was your encouragement for effort that instilled in the child courage to try again. How sad that we forget this technique of creative teaching as the child gets older. We walk into Sophie's room and see that twelve toys are on the floor. We calmly ask Sophie to please put her toys in the toy box. We go back in five minutes. Seven toys are in the box, and five are on the floor. We have an option. We can give condemning words, such as, "I told you, Sophie, to get these toys in the toy box." Or we can choose encouraging words: "Yeah! Seven in the box." I bet the other five will jump into the box. Encouraging words motivate positive behavior; condemning words stifle effort.

Several years ago, I went to the hospital to visit a thirteen-year-old boy who had stomach ulcers. In an effort to discover the emotional dynamics in his life, I asked the question, "How do you get along with your father?"

He replied, "Not very well."

"Can you give me some examples?" I asked.

"If I make a B on my report card," he said, "my father always says, 'You should have made an A. You are smarter than that.' If I am playing ball and I get a double, my father says, 'You should have made a triple out of that. Can't you run?' If I mow the grass, when I get through, my father always finds something wrong with my job such as, 'You didn't get under the bushes. Can't you see the grass under the bushes?' I don't ever do anything right."

I knew the boy's father. By all objective standards, he would have been considered a good father. I knew his intentions. He was trying to communicate to his son, "When you play ball, give it your best. When you go to school, live up to your potential. When you do a job, do it right." No doubt he remembered the words of his own father, who said, "If a job is worth doing, it's worth doing right." The father was trying to stimulate his son to excellence in every area of life, but do you understand what his son was hearing? "I don't ever do anything right." The father's well-meaning words had served as a source of discouragement to the teenage son and created deep emotional turmoil within.

The time to help a child bring a B to an A is not the day he brings the report card home. That's the day to praise the child for the B. Three days later, when the report card is back on the teacher's desk, then the parent can say, "Michael, you did a good job. You made a B in math. What do you think we could do to bring that B up to an A next quarter?" Your praise for past effort will likely encourage him to pursue the higher goal. The time to teach the child to stretch the double into a triple is not the day he makes the double. That's the day to scream your praise from the sidelines: "Yeah! A double!" Two afternoons later, you can show him in the backyard how to slide into third and stretch the double into a triple. The time to teach a child to mow under the bushes is not the day he finishes mowing the grass. That's the day to praise him for the grass mowed. "Hey, Mike, good job, man! Lots of hard work. The yard looks great. Thanks for mowing the yard." Next Saturday when he begins to mow the grass again, the father can say, "Michael, see this grass under the bushes? It's difficult to get. You have to go in and out, but I am sure you can do it. You're doing a great job." I can almost guarantee you the grass under the bushes will be leveled. Children respond to encouraging words. Such words instill courage to reach out to accomplish greater levels of potential. In a healthy family, encouraging words are a way of life.

When our children were young and we moved from one house to another, I discovered the following letter while I was rummaging through some old boxes. I had written it to Derek after he had experienced a rather discouraging day at basketball scrimmage.

Dear Derek:

I know that last night's scrimmage was a great disappointment to you, and rightfully so. Anytime we don't perform up to the level we know we can, it is discouraging. A setback in reaching our goals is always hard. I know, because I have had a few myself.

This morning, I was thinking about biblical characters who had setbacks: (1) Joseph when his brothers sold him into slavery, (2) Joseph when Potiphar's wife falsely accused him, (3) Abraham when he lied and said that his wife was his sister, (4) Peter when he denied that he knew Christ. I know that they must have felt badly with their setbacks too. But all of them went on to become great men for God.

I know that you are not a quitter. I know you will bounce back and give it your best. But I wanted you to know that I understand your discouragement.

I love you very much and I'm proud of you no matter how you play. You have character and that is what really counts—in ball and in life!!!

Love,
Dad

Encouraging words, written or spoken, live in the minds of children long after they are forgotten by the parents who spoke them.

CREATIVE CORRECTION

The third area of creative teaching is creative correction. In a loving family, parents give correction when needed. But it is important that correction be given creatively. Remember: our goal is to teach in such a way as to whet the appetite. We want to stimulate the child to positive behavior. Correction can be given negatively or positively. Let's look at a positive pattern of correction.

First of all, we must make sure that we are not correcting behavior that doesn't need to be corrected. In our efforts to teach our children, we sometimes stifle creativity in favor of conformity. Creativity is the wonderful gift of thinking outside the lines. It is our creativity that allows us to develop the uniqueness implanted within each of us. To stifle this creativity is to make children look like cookies rather than snowflakes. Dr. Howard Hendricks, national speaker on the subject of creativity, tells of the child who drew flowers with faces. The teacher said, "Johnny, flowers don't have faces."

Johnny replied, "Mine do!" Johnny's creativity is still alive, but if his teacher succeeds, his flowers will eventually look like everyone else's flowers. In a healthy family, we are seeking to correct only those kinds of behavior that are destructive and detrimental to the child's development. We are not trying to destroy the child's unique expressions of creativity.

A good question for the parent to ask is, "Is the behavior I am about to correct truly destructive to my child? Will it be detrimental to his future if I allow it to continue?" If the answer is yes, then correction is in order. If the answer is no or if you are uncertain, then it is time to explore the child's behavior further. Perhaps you will find an opportunity to encourage the developing of creativity and imagination. For example, the teacher might have responded to Johnny's flower with a face by asking Johnny to explain what the flower is saying. Johnny could then use his imagination to express a message that would likely reveal something of his own thoughts and feelings and give the teacher much insight into what is going on inside Johnny's mind. Asking questions before we decide to give correction is a safeguard that healthy parents have learned.

Assuming correction is needed, we must correct out of love, not out of uncontrolled anger. Love seeks the well-being of the child and believes that the correction given is for the long-term benefit of the child. Expressions of uncontrolled anger are simply the venting of our own frustration and may be extremely destructive to the child. I am not suggesting that a parent should never feel anger toward a child; that is unrealistic. Anger is the emotion that arises inside us when we perceive that the child has done wrong, such as when he refuses to follow our instruction or interprets our "no" as a "maybe" that could turn into a "yes" if he pleads with us long enough.

Anger is a perfectly normal and often wholesome emotion. Its purpose is to motivate us to take constructive action; however, parents often allow their anger to go unchecked and end up with destructive words and behavior. If you feel anger toward your child and believe that the child needs correction, you will do far better to restrain your initial response, give yourself time to cool down, and then come back to verbally correct the child and to give further discipline if needed.

Love asks the essential question, "Is the correction I am about to give for the benefit of my child (or the entire family/community)?" It is this reality that must be communicated to the child in our efforts to correct. "I love you a lot. I love you a whole lot. And I want to see you live to adulthood. Therefore, you must never again ride your bicycle without a helmet. Understand?" If, after this loving correction, you hand the child a newspaper clipping of a teenager who was killed when thrown from a bicycle, you are likely to have a helmet-wearing child forever.

Creative correction must also seek to explain. Typically, tongue-lashing does not correct behavior. Rather, it ostracizes children. As soon as the child is old enough to understand, we should seek to explain the wrong behavior and give instruction for the future. Our purpose is not to humiliate the child by calling him names; our purpose is to correct the child so that he can become a responsible individual. To call a child "stupid" reveals more about our own intelligence than it does about the child's. No thinking adult would wish to communicate such an idea to a child. This does not mean that if we have reverted to such name-calling, we are forever dysfunctional parents. It does mean that we must take action to confess our wrongdoing to the child. "I am sorry I lost my temper, and I am especially sorry that I called you 'stupid' because that is not true. You are a very intelligent person. I am the one who was unwise in using that word. I was upset, and I failed to get control of myself before I started talking. I want to ask you to forgive me. I want to help you become an even wiser person than you are now, and I want to continue learning how to be a good father." These are the words of a wise father indeed. Children are willing to forgive failure if we are willing to admit it.

The third principle of creative correction is that we deal only with the matter at hand. We do not bring up past failures. To parade before a child all of his past failures before you correct him for his current failure is to communicate that he must indeed be a failure. How many times did Edison fail before he invented the lightbulb? No one calls Edison a failure, although he failed far more often than he succeeded. Your child may be an Edison. Don't discourage him by parading his past failures before him.

To parents who tend to be perfectionistic, I must add this warning: please do not expect perfection of your children. Machines may perform perfectly, at least if everything is in operating order, but your child is not a machine. He or she is a human, filled with potential and pitfalls. It is the task of the parent to help the child avoid the pitfalls in an effort to reach his or her potential. We do this best not by demanding perfection, but by encouraging effort and making corrections when needed.

Lending courage to try again is far more productive than saying, "Well, you failed again. Why don't you just quit?" or "Let me do it for you." The "let me do it for you" philosophy of parenting produces fearful, passive, nonproductive children. When parents "take charge," they stifle the child's initiative to learn. Remember, our task as parents is not to get the job done; our task is to whet the appetite of our children so that they will be highly motivated to experience the joy of learning and become productive adults.

If the child tends to be easily discouraged in his efforts and seems to be overly sensitive to criticism, parents may wish to expose him to the biographies of people like Thomas Edison, Helen Keller, Babe Ruth, and George Washington Carver, who stand as monuments of what can be accomplished through failure. Failure is our friend, not our enemy. Every failure teaches us another way not to do it. With new insight, we come closer to the truth. Through such biographies, children's perception of failure may be turned in a positive direction.

CREATIVE AFFIRMATION

The fourth area of creative teaching is creative affirmation. Verbal affirmation of our children differs from encouraging words in that words of encouragement are typically tied to the actions of the child, whereas affirmation is affirming the child himself. "I love you. You are wonderful. I like your hair. Your eyes are beautiful. You have a sharp mind. You are tall and handsome. You are strong" are all affirming words about who the child is. In healthy families, the parents seek to develop healthy self-esteem by pointing out positive attributes of the child's personality, body, or mind. Affirmation is accentuating the positive. We are not ignoring the negative, but we are seeking to affirm the child in an effort to overcome the negative messages that he or she will receive from peers and from self-analysis.

Today's children compare themselves with the athletic and photogenic models seen on TV and social media. By these perfected standards, almost all children come up short. It is the parents' task to help the child develop healthy self-esteem in a world that has exalted the beautiful, the brainy, and the athletic and has left the rest of us average citizens wallowing in feelings of inferiority. As parents we must offset this imbalance.

"Of all the words I say to you, what do you like to hear most of all?" a mother asked her eight-year-old son.

"When you tell me how strong I am," he replied, with a smile creeping across his face. In this brief conversation, a mother has learned the power of affirming words. Parents who are teaching creatively will seek to affirm the worth of their children by giving verbal affirmation.

CHAPTER SEVEN

The Challenge of Consistent Training

In my personal study of anthropology, I have never observed a culture where parents are not expected to provide children with guidance. The biological reality is that the human child is born virtually helpless. Left alone, the infant will most certainly die. Nurturing begins with the first tender touch of a mother nursing her baby. Research is abundantly clear that babies who are touched and cuddled develop healthier feelings of security than babies who receive little tactile contact. Thus, child guidance by parental action begins in the early hours of a child's life. In our society, it continues for at least eighteen years.

We have eighteen years to take a child from the state of total dependence to a state of relative independence. In functional families, parents recognize and readily accept this responsibility of training. Such training usually requires more time than verbal instruction. *Telling* a child how to do something is easier and less time-consuming than *showing* the child how to do it, observing her behavior, and making further recommendations for improvement.

This process of training involves not only training in certain skills, such as reading, writing, bathing, and riding a bicycle, but it also involves teaching the child how to respond to such emotions as fear, anger, and disappointment. It involves character development with an emphasis on such fundamental values as honesty, hard work, and courage. If such work is demanding for parents, it is also rewarding. The payoff is in the quality of life the child lives, and the side benefit is that the child's training positively affects the society at large. As Dr. Karl Menninger once said, "What's done to children, they will do to society."[1] The training of children is indeed a noble pursuit. How then do we succeed at such an awesome responsibility?

WE TRAIN BY OUR MODEL

Let's begin at the beginning. Our children learn first and primarily by our model. They are forever observing our actions, our lifestyle. If what we say is not consistent with what we do, they are the first to recognize it and usually to tell us so. Someone has suggested that until a boy is fifteen, he does what his father says; after that, he does what his father does. This is both a frightening and a wonderful thought for most parents. It is frightening to know that we have such a tremendous impact upon the lives of our children, but it is encouraging to realize that whatever we know or don't know about parenting, if we live lives worthy of emulation, we will powerfully influence our children in a positive direction. Abraham Lincoln is attributed to have said, "I regard no man as poor who has had a godly mother."[2] Who we are speaks loudly to our children and is perhaps our most powerful method of training.

Let me give a personal example. Through all my early childhood years, my father worked the third shift in a textile mill, going to work at 11:00 p.m. and getting off at 7:00 a.m. Each morning as I was preparing to go to school, he was preparing to go to bed. A part of his morning pattern was to pray, either kneeling by the bed or in the bathroom. My father had the habit of praying aloud. I don't mean screaming, but in a normal voice he prayed aloud. As

I shuffled from my room to the kitchen, I often heard him pray. Sometimes, I heard him pray for me. I knew praying was important to him, and it became important to me. It became so important that my undergraduate and graduate studies in anthropology, philosophy, and history, all of which had little place for prayer, did not erase my own personal commitment to my father's model.

I do not mean to convey that our model will determine the practices of our children throughout life. Determinism is not consistent with man's freedom. I do mean to say that our model will have a powerful influence upon our children and that, in fact, the influence of our model will never be forgotten. The most sober question that has ever crossed my mind as a parent is this: "What if my children turn out to be like me?" That question has made many hard moral choices easier. I do not claim to have attained this, but it is my clear goal to live my life in such a way that I would not be embarrassed if my choices were copied by my children.

This does not mean that children cannot learn from a negative model. At the risk of boring you with my own life (how could that be possible?), let me again be personal. My grandfather was an alcoholic. He, too, worked in a textile mill, but after many years of seniority, he worked the first shift, going to work at 7:00 a.m. and getting off at 3:00 p.m. It appeared to me as a ten-year-old that he lived for the weekends and he lived to drink. Every Friday afternoon, he walked the half mile to Goat Turners, the local hangout for men his age. He drank till dark and then tried to walk home.

On numerous occasions, someone in the neighborhood would knock on our door, call my father to the door, and tell him that his father had fallen in the ditch and needed help. On several occasions, I accompanied my father, pulling my grandfather out of the ditch, walking him home on our shoulders, giving him a bath, and putting him to bed. As a young teenager, I lost all desire for alcohol, and I confess readily that I have never had a temptation to drink. As an older adult myself, I now recognize that that decision has saved me thousands of dollars over the years and has likely saved my life. I owe all those benefits to my grandfather. His model spoke loudly, and I got the message.

Those of you who grew up with what you consider to be poor parental models, and who have read the research that indicates that children of alcoholics are more likely to become alcoholics, children of abusive parents are more likely to abuse, and so forth, take heart. Personal individual freedom is a reality. Although you may be psychologically and physically more prone to the behavior modeled by your parents, it is not necessary for you to repeat their destructive lifestyles. Your choice to walk another path, the encouragement of friends, and the help of God can influence you in the opposite direction. You can become a functional parent from a dysfunctional family. One of the marvelous traits of being human is that we can change our direction in life.

Our choice to change becomes a positive model for our children. I remember the day my father stopped smoking. We were painting a room together. His hacking cough had become increasingly acute. He was on the ladder when he reached in his pocket for another cigarette, but instead of lighting it, he twisted it, and threw it to the floor. He reached for the remaining half pack in his pocket, twisted the entire pack, threw it to the floor, and said, "That's the last cigarette I will ever smoke. I don't need those things." He never smoked again. I have always admired him for that decision. He demonstrated for me the reality of human freedom to choose the higher road, and he trained me by his model.

WE TRAIN BY SHOWING HOW

He was only six years old (I know his age because he told me), with blond hair and blue eyes, and he was excited. I guessed his father to be in his late twenties or early thirties. They were the only ones on the lake before I arrived. They didn't know me and I didn't know them, but Brent, the six-year-old, was eager to show me the fish he had caught and to inform me that his father was teaching him how to fish. His father smiled affirmingly, and after a few more oohs and aahs about Brent's catch, I walked on around the lake knowing that I had been privileged to observe a live session in parental training.

It is possible to sit in the living room with your child and tell him how to go fishing, but it is far more effective to take him to the lake and show him how. Football teams can watch video clips and devise strategies and better understand their opponents, but the real skills are learned on the practice field. Making beds, washing dishes, mopping floors, and washing cars are all best learned by on-the-job training.

Much of preschool parental education falls into the category of training by showing them how. We teach them to count marbles or apples by touching the objects as we say, "One, two, three, four . . ." Before long they are touching the objects and saying, "One, two, three, four . . ." When our daughter, Shelley, came along, the current rage was "Teach your child to read" before sending him or her off to school. Karolyn made flash cards with the words *toes, knee, nose, hand, door, apple, orange,* etc. Several times a day, Shelley would call for the flash cards and want to "read." Before long, she was recognizing these words in storybooks that we read together, and before she went off to school, she was indeed reading. Karolyn taught her by "showing her how."

In virtually all cultures, children are taught the basic skills of life by their parents. Whether it is hunting monkeys, planting yams, or finding berries, parents show them how.

WE TRAIN BY WEAVING ACTIONS WITH WORDS

E. V. Hill, the late pastor of a large congregation in South Central Los Angeles, tells this story from his own life. He was in his early teens when he came home one night drunk. As he walked into his room, he threw up all over the floor. In a drunken stupor, he rolled onto his bed and fell asleep. His mother, observing the whole scene, let him sleep. At the proper morning hour, however, E. V. was awakened with his mother's instruction. "E. V., get up. Get this floor cleaned up. Get yourself cleaned up. You and I are going on a trip."

"I don't want to go on a trip," E. V. said.

His mother said, "I didn't ask if you wanted to go on a trip. I said, 'You and I are going on a trip.' Now get this floor cleaned up and get yourself cleaned up."

E. V. started the process and in due time was ready for his trip. In the late morning, he and his mother boarded the subway for a destination unknown to E. V. Emerging from the station, he found himself on Skid Row. His mother cooked at one of the rescue missions two nights a week, so many of the men on Skid Row knew her. As the mother and son walked down the sidewalk, the men greeted her. "Good afternoon, Mama Hill."

One man asked, "Why are you here so early?"

She replied, "This is my son, E. V. He took up drinking, and he's planning to live down here. I wanted him to come down and see it before dark."

Pastor Hill testified, "That's the last time I ever drank alcohol." His mother was an effective trainer (weaving actions with words). A lecture on the evils of alcohol would not have had the same effect.

Whether we are correcting behavior we believe to be destructive or teaching children history or morals, actions tied with words are more effective than words alone. For example, let's say that you are teaching your children something of the history of America and you want them to know the religious moral roots of our nation. It is possible to give them a lecture, and it is also possible to expose them to history books. But would that have the same effect as taking a train to Washington, DC, standing at the south wall of the Lincoln Memorial, and reading Lincoln's own words inscribed into the granite walls? "That this nation, under God, shall have a new birth of freedom; and that government of the people, by the people, for the people, shall not perish from the earth."

The family exploring Washington, DC, could also walk to the north wall and read: "As was said some 3,000 years ago, so still it must be said, 'The judgments of the Lord are true and righteous altogether.'" They could visit the Jefferson Memorial on the south banks of Washington's Tidal Basin and read Jefferson's words: "No man shall . . . suffer on account of his religious opinions or belief, but all men shall be free to profess and by argument to maintain, their opinion in matters of religion."

The specific words of the inscriptions may be forgotten, but the visual image of standing at the base of the monument with his family reading those words will always be a positive memory. And if the student took notes on the inscriptions, when he writes a high school paper, you are likely to see him pulling out his old notes and including them in his history paper.

Whatever you are trying to teach, it is helpful to ask the question, "What could I do with my child that might make this lesson more effective?" Children learn best by doing. If you want your children to know the tragic reality of man's inhumanity to man, take them to the Holocaust Museum in Washington, DC, or in Israel. They will never forget the experience.

Weaving of actions and words is extremely effective in training children. This is true in both the teaching of skills and the molding of character. Doing things with your children, even if there is no specific educational objective, is in fact teaching your children the value of relationships. In functional families, parents and children do things together. Sometimes these activities have specific educational goals in mind. Other times, they are simply "for fun," but all family activities are in fact times of training for children. Perhaps most basically, we are giving them a model of parenting that emphasizes that parents and children are family and families do things together.

Using your creativity to make these "together times" also "learning times" can be a real challenge, but the rewards are lasting. Even the mundane can be turned into a fun learning experience if you are creative. One family told me that when it comes time to clean the house, they pretend that the family is a professional cleaning service cleaning someone else's house. They organize themselves and assign responsibilities. A supervisor, typically one of the parents (but it could be an older teenager), makes sure that each job is done "up to quality." At the appointed time, they get an official break and everyone gets a treat. When the task is completed, they take a walk together and discuss what they learned about life from their housecleaning job.

"The children often learn things we didn't intend to teach," the mother said. "For example, there was the time our nine-year-old son said, 'I discovered that if you don't leave hairs in the sink, then it's easier for the person who must clean the sink.' Not a lesson we intended to teach, but one we're certainly glad he learned. And in fact from that time on, he always got the hairs out of the sink every time he left the bathroom."

In a loving family, parents give guidance to their children by consistent training from infancy through adolescence. Our own model—intentional or unintentional—is our most effective method of training.

LEARNING TO TEACH AND TRAIN

I can hear some parents saying, "Hold it. Stop the train. I want to get off. My parents weren't educated, but they just loved us, and we turned out all right. So why make such a big deal of it? Aren't we making parenting too hard?"

I must confess I have some sympathy for these thoughts. But

there are some very real reasons that today's parents must be far more intentional in the parenting process. In the traditional pattern of the first hundred and fifty years of the United States—and in nonliterate cultures—culture was far more homogenous. An accepted pattern of life was held by the general populace. Right was right and wrong was wrong, and most people agreed about what fell into each category. Parents, the school, the church, and the neighbors all agreed on proper behavior for children, and each reinforced the other. If parents loved their children and provided for their physical needs and "did what came naturally" in parenting their children, the children probably did turn out all right. A part of that family pattern involved parental authority; children were taught to respect their parents and other adults. Since everyone was teaching the child the same principles, it was not difficult for the child to understand and learn to live within that framework.

However, today's world is radically different. We have no system of thought or accepted lifestyle upon which all of society agrees. The messages that vie for the child's attention are often contradictory. The lifestyle of the neighbor next door (or even at church) may be radically different from the lifestyle in the child's family. The child may become extremely confused; thus, parental guidance is more essential than in a former age.

What remains true in all societies is that parents have the primary responsibility for teaching and training their own children. In spite of the fact that in Western contemporary culture the school has become a major player, in my opinion parents must not abdicate this responsibility. Who will interpret the messages the child hears at school, on TV, online, at church, and in the neighborhood? I believe that is the parents' responsibility. For those of us in the Judeo-Christian tradition who believe that the Ten Commandments serve as a basis for society's moral fiber, our role as parents becomes exceedingly important in the modern pluralistic society. Thus, it is true that the demands of parenting are far greater today than in a past generation. We can no longer simply do what comes naturally with our children. The modern child is far too exposed to dangerous and destructive lifestyles. If we truly love our children, we are compelled to teach and train them in keeping with the principles we believe to be true. This chapter is for those of you who sincerely want to sharpen your skills at teaching and training your children.

BRING IT HOME

I know I am writing to many who are highly skilled at teaching and training. Some of you are professional teachers and have not only an academic background in education, but some years in teaching in public or private schools. Some of you have been homeschooling for years. Others of you are in professions that have required long and strenuous programs of formal education. If you have finished college and perhaps graduate school, you are most keenly aware that some people are good teachers and some are in professional positions as teachers who have never developed the skills of teaching. Perhaps you have learned from a negative example how not to teach. Some of you are in the medical profession, which has an extensive history in the weaving of training by action and teaching by instruction.

Most of my readers will have gained some skills in life, and chances are at least some of those skills were learned in teaching or training settings. You have learned numerous skills that you apply in your vocation and in your other professional relationships. What has always amazed me is how few people bring these skills back into the family. It is as though in our efforts to separate "work" and "family," we have so compartmentalized the two that we have failed to bring the benefit of the one to the other. For example, I have talked to many executives who have learned the skill of reflective listening in which they regularly say to colleagues or customers such statements or questions as, "What I hear you saying is . . ." or "Are you saying . . . ?" and who find this simple technique of communication extremely helpful in their profession—but who have never sought to use this skill in relating to their children.

Therefore, the first challenge is to identify the skills in teaching and training that you have already learned in life and bring these home, letting your children be the beneficiaries of your learning. What have you learned in your vocation or in your community involvement that could be transferred to the teaching and training of your children? For example, some of you use PowerPoint presentations in your vocation. Have you ever used PowerPoint in explaining something to your children? You have learned that treating other people's ideas as worthy of consideration is the sign of wisdom in the workplace. Is that any less true in family relationships? Hearing a person out before responding is commonplace in the life of many professionals, and you probably have learned that skill. But do your children have a sense that they are heard, or do they have the sense that you are operating under the adage "Children are to be seen, not heard"?

Why not sit down with your spouse and make a list of all the skills each of you has learned through the years in how to relate to people, how to communicate information, how to lead people in decision-making, how to train people in skills, and so forth. Make a list of these, being as descriptive as you can with each skill. Then decide which of these you might seek to use this week with your children to be a more effective teacher or trainer.

GO GET IT

Some of you are young parents. You have not had a lot of experience in teaching and training. Your vocation may not require a lot of transferable skills. You honestly have very little idea how children learn, and, thus, you have little idea how parents can effectively teach and train. You may feel inept, even frightened, at this awesome responsibility. The good news is that practical help is readily available.

It does require time and sometimes the investment of a little money, but thousands of parents can testify to the effectiveness of formal education in learning to teach and train children.

Most community colleges provide courses with such titles as: Child Development, How Children Learn, Understanding Teenagers, or Principles of Effective Teaching. The practicality of these classes will obviously depend upon the effectiveness of the teacher and the educational philosophy behind the course. But many of these courses can be helpful to the discerning parent.

Many churches are now offering parenting classes that focus on various aspects of teaching and training children. Even with classes geared to teaching children in the church setting, the principles of teaching and training can be readily transferred to the home. These courses often focus on the various age groups, such as teaching preschoolers, teaching children, or teaching teenagers. Some courses are designed to give basic skills for teaching and training, while others focus on practical ideas for how to teach particular skills and how to deal with specific developmental problems. One woman told me, "I never knew that other parents had trouble with potty training until I attended a class at my church in preschool education. I took ideas from other parents and the instructor, went home, changed my approach, and was amazed by the results."

It was in such a class, focusing on music and children, that my wife was first impressed with the value of music as a teaching tool. She bought numerous musical records (flat, black, round, with little grooves), and our early American turntable became the center of many hours of teaching and training the children. Contemporary parents have smartphones; you can even teach with music while you drive rather than listening to the news or music on the radio.

In any area of parenting where you feel deficient, I can almost guarantee that somewhere, someone is teaching a class that will give you practical help. Your struggles in parenting are common to other parents. They only seem unique when you parent alone. Colleges, churches, synagogues, and various civic groups all offer courses for parents. Reach out for help—go get it!

OBSERVE OTHERS

Much can be learned about teaching and training children by observing teachers and trainers. Watch other parents in action. Almost any social setting will give you an opportunity to see parents relating to children. The supermarket, the library, the church, the mall, and the restaurant are all settings where parents and children interact. Observe both the positive and the negative interactions between parent and child. Perhaps you will want to get a notebook where you can write these observations down and reflect upon them later. Keep in mind that you can learn from negative examples of teaching and training as well as from positive examples.

The informal settings described above allow you to observe parents in a casual format. The parent may not be consciously teaching or training the child. (In reality, of course, parents are always teaching and training.) You can also learn from observing intentional settings for learning. Consider visiting a classroom at your child's school. If your children are not yet school age, perhaps you could visit the classroom of the child of a friend of yours. Observe the teacher in action. Watch the verbal interactions between teacher and pupils and observe the actions the teacher takes. Note the way words, actions, and visual aids are woven together in the classroom setting. Or visit your child's Sunday school room and observe the teacher or teachers in action. You may want to volunteer to sit in on a preschool class once a month if your child is a preschooler. In many churches, teachers have been trained in the learning styles of preschoolers. I have personally been extremely encouraged by the quality of teaching and training that goes on in the preschool department of the church I attend. Parents could learn much from watching these teachers.

If you are still in college or you attend classes at a local educational institution, observe your own teachers. The methods they use with you may not translate directly to the teaching and training of your children, but with some modification, you may pick up some excellent ideas. On the other hand, you may get classic examples on "how not to teach." One of my most vivid memories of graduate school is a professor who sat at the end of a long table with seven graduate school students sitting around the table listening to him read from his notes written on paper yellowed by age. He droned on for the entire class period, and at the beginning of class he often needed five minutes to find his place before he could start reading again. It didn't take long for me to learn that this was not the way to teach anyone anything.

Another place to observe skilled teachers is on some children's TV programs. Obviously, the teacher may have more colorful props than are available to you in the home, but look for the teaching style and the way words and actions are used to teach children. Some children's programming is an excellent source to observe creative teaching methods. You may also incorporate these programs as a part of your own teaching—but if you do, do so deliberately and not as a way to "babysit" the children and reassure yourself that they're learning.

By all means, ask questions of other parents about how they teach and train their children. If you are personal friends with schoolteachers or Sunday school teachers, these people are usually excited about comparing ideas with parents on how to creatively teach children. Keeping a notebook on what you observe and writing down your own ideas and thoughts in response to what you see can make your observations more meaningful. Perhaps you pick up an especially creative idea for teaching fifth-grade children, but your child is only three years old. If you don't write it down, you will have forgotten it by the time he gets to the fifth grade.

READ A BOOK

Another excellent source for developing your teaching and training skills is reading a book or researching online. Fortunately, many books are available. Parenting websites abound. Some books are geared to teaching specific age groups, such as preschoolers three to five years of age. Others are written to give more basic principles of the teaching and learning process. Both can be helpful. A visit to your local public library or to the library of your church will likely reveal an abundance of resources from which you can choose. Not all are of equal value, so it may be helpful to ask the advice of a teacher. Most teachers are eager to discuss resources with interested parents.

One warning: Do not become so obsessed by reading books on how to be a parent that you don't have time left over to actually parent. I have observed some parents who are so keen on the idea of educating themselves on being a parent that their children go neglected. By the time the child is leaving home, the parents are excellent educators. Unfortunately, we only get one chance to raise our children. Therefore, we must learn as we go.

For more information on how you can better love and guide your children well, see the code on page 177 to access the Family Adventure Guide at **www.5lovelanguages.com/5traits**. This guide is to help put into practice the healthy traits discussed in this book. You'll find a number of assessments, things to think about, and opportunities for deeper discussion.

PART FOUR

Children Who Obey and Honor Parents

Why Obedience Matters

It was 4:30 in the afternoon. My then ten-year-old son and I were standing in the den where I was saying, "I'm sorry, son, but you cannot ride your bicycle this afternoon. You know the rule. The bicycle is to be placed in the storage shed every night. If you leave it out, then you do not get to ride the bicycle the following day. Last night you left it out all night; therefore, you cannot ride the bike this afternoon."

Derek replied, "But, Dad, all the guys are riding this afternoon. Let me ride today and I won't ride tomorrow."

I told him, "I understand that you really want to ride the bike today. But you and I both agreed on the rule and on the consequences. I'm sorry; you can't ride the bike today. I understand; this is hard on you. It hurts when you can't go riding with your friends, but you must learn to put the bike in the storage shed each night."

I envisioned John, our live-in anthropologist, standing in the living room listening to this conversation. Many thoughts were running through my mind: Would he think I am being harsh, cruel, unbending? Or would he understand that I am loving my son, that it hurts me as much as it hurts him not to see him riding his bike with his friends? I didn't really know how John would read the situation, but I knew that what I was doing was the hard work of teaching obedience.

This is harder and harder for parents today. We live in an increasingly egalitarian culture where everyone is presumed to have the same "rights." Respect for authority, whether in the workplace, at school, or in the church, has ebbed as people have become more cynical about their leaders. Beyond societal influences, today's busy, tired parent often finds it easier to let little Jacob or Caitlin stay up late or eat junk food.

It is true that some parents abuse authority. However, the greater danger is to raise a child who grows up without the limits they so desperately need. In a healthy and loving family, parental authority is used for the benefit of the children. The parents are committed to high ethical and moral standards. They espouse the virtues of kindness, love, honesty, forgiveness, integrity, hard work, and treating others with respect. Children who obey such parents will reap the benefit of living under wholesome authority.

LOVE AND OBEDIENCE

Just as societies and nations need laws and rules to function, so every family must establish and abide by certain rules. It is our love for each other, our desire for the well-being of each other, and our fear of the consequences that motivates us to obedience.

Obedience, however, is something that must be learned. We are not born with an obedience gene; rather, it seems that we are born with a disposition to test the rules and push the boundaries. Who has not watched a two-year-old inch his fingers toward a forbidden object, waiting to see if his parents will respond? Obedience is learned, and it is learned best when the child genuinely feels loved by the parents. That is, when the child is deeply convinced that the parents care about his or her well-being. If the child is convinced that the parents do not love him, that they care only for themselves and have set out to make his life miserable, the child may comply outwardly with the rules, but inwardly the child is rebelling. In due time this rebellion will surface in blatant disobedience.

The other factor in learning obedience is experiencing the reality that all behavior will have consequences. Obedient behavior brings positive consequences; disobedient behavior brings negative consequences. It is this consistent reality that teaches the child the value of obedience. Thus, in a loving family, the parents will focus on these two realities: loving the child and making every effort to know that the child feels loved, and making sure that the child experiences the consequences of his or her behavior. This process involves three things: setting rules, setting consequences (good as well as bad), and administering discipline. Let's examine these three.

GOOD RULES, BAD RULES

To do or not to do, that is the nature of rules. Rules give guidelines for family living. These are things we do not do in our family: chew gum at the table, bounce a basketball in the kitchen, leave the house with candles burning, jump on the sofa, or mistreat the dog. These are things we do in our family: put tools away when we have finished using them, put toys away when we have finished playing with them, turn lights off when we leave the room, say "may I be excused" when we leave the dinner table, bring our dirty clothes to the laundry room, call and let Mom or Dad know where we are.

Sometimes rules are confusing, such as "Always turn the lights out when you leave the house except when Grandma is still awake or the dog is sick or when you know your brother is playing in the backyard." With such a rule, the only safe thing is don't ever leave the house. Sometimes rules are unstated, as they were for the fifteen-year-old who said, "One rule at my house is 'Don't ever talk to Dad when he's drunk.'"

"Did your mother tell you this rule?" I asked.

"No, I learned it from experience," he said.

All families have rules, but not all families have healthy rules. Good rules have four characteristics: they are intentional, they are mutual; they are reasonable, and they are discussed with the entire family.

Intentional rules are those to which we have given conscious thought. They do not simply emerge from our own frustration at the moment, but they have come with considerable thought as to why the rule is needed, what the purpose of the rule is, and whether it is really for the benefit of everyone. Intentional rules mean that we don't have a rule simply because it was a rule in our own families. For example, many families have the rule, "We don't sing at the table." Upon inquiry as to why a family has this rule, often the answer is "That's the way it was at my house." Now, I ask, "What is so bad about singing at the table?" I'm not suggesting that it is a bad rule or a good rule; I'm simply asking, "Why do you have the rule? What are you trying to accomplish by this rule?" Making rules intentionally means that we think about each of our rules and thus do not become captive to some meaningless tradition.

Second, good rules involve mutual input of the father and the mother. Each of us grew up in different families; consequently, we had different rules. I tend to bring my rules to my family, and my wife tends to bring her rules. If these rules do not agree, we often have conflicts over the rules. These conflicts should be handled like all other marital conflicts. We should hear each other out, treat each other's ideas with dignity and respect, tell our honest thoughts and feelings, and, if we cannot agree, ask ourselves, "Then what can we agree on?" and look for an alternative in the middle of our two ideas. For example, if I believe that a sixteen-year-old should be in at 11:00 and my wife believes that he should be in at 10:00, then perhaps we can agree on 10:30. If you believe children's intentional burping is utterly uncivilized and your husband thinks it's cute, perhaps you can disallow it in the house and the car but permit it in the backyard.

EVALUATING RULES

In a healthy marriage, parents respect each other's ideas and neither is dictatorial in rule making. The ideas and feelings of both should be considered in setting rules for the family. As the children get older, they should be brought into the decision-making process. If the rule applies to them and they are old enough to have an opinion on the subject, then they should be allowed to be a part of setting the rule. That doesn't mean that they have the final word, but it does mean that parents should consider their thoughts and feelings. When families do this, parents are not only teaching kids the importance of obedience; they are also teaching them the process of setting rules.

Healthy rules are also reasonable. They serve some positive function. The overarching questions are, "Is this rule good for the child? Will it have some positive effect on the child's life?" The following are some practical questions to ask as you decide about a particular rule.

Does this rule keep the child from danger or destruction?

Does this rule teach the child some positive character trait: honesty, hard work, kindness, sharing, etc.?

Does this rule protect property?

Does this rule teach stewardship of possessions?

Does this rule teach the child responsibility?

Does this rule teach good manners?

In answering questions like these, we are far more likely to come up with healthy rules for the family. These are the factors about which we are concerned as parents. We want to keep our children from danger and destruction. We do not want our young child to be hit by a car in the street, and we do not want our older children to get involved in drugs. We want to teach our children positive character traits in keeping with our values. We want children to respect the property of others; thus, a rule about not playing baseball in the backyard may well keep them from breaking a neighbor's window.

107

We want them to learn to take care of their own possessions; thus, the rule about putting the bicycle in the storage shed at night is a purposeful rule.

We want our children to be responsible adults, and we know that they must learn this in childhood. Therefore, requiring a child to be responsible for making his bed or vacuuming his floor are reasonable rules. And what of good manners? It is interesting that contemporary corporate executives are hiring etiquette trainers and consultants because the social graces of contemporary employees are so greatly characterized by rudeness and crudeness. I believe this can be traced to the lack of teaching manners in the home. If a parent believes that "please" and "thank you" are better than "gimme" and "yuck," then he will have rules regarding such manners in the home.

Reasonable rules always have a positive purpose. Healthy rules are also clearly stated. Parents often assume that children know what they are to do or not to do when expectations have never been explained to the child. Once parents have agreed on a rule, the entire family needs to be made aware of it. Unspoken rules are unfair rules. A child cannot be expected to live up to a standard of which he is unaware. Parents have the responsibility for making sure that children understand what the rules are. As children grow older, they need to know why their parents have decided on this rule. If children feel genuinely loved by the parents, they will usually acknowledge the value of such rules. In making family rules, it is perfectly legitimate to consult other parents, schoolteachers, and extended families and to read books and articles. To have the best possible rules, parents need all the wisdom they can get.

Good family rules are not set in concrete. If you come to see that a particular rule is detrimental rather than helpful, then you should be willing to change that rule. In our family, we started out with the rule of no singing at the table. We quickly realized that this rule was a product of our families of origin and did not fit our view of what a mealtime should be. With my wife being a musician and me having a deep appreciation for music, we quickly concluded that that rule needed to be abandoned and that anyone who wanted to break forth in song at our table was welcome to do so (as long as there was no food in the person's mouth).

To evaluate your family rules, begin by writing the name and age of each child at the top of a separate sheet of paper. Underneath each child's name, list the rules that you think the family has already made that apply to that child. You may want to make two categories of rules: first, rules that apply to all the children and, second, specific rules that apply to each child because of his or her developmental stage or special interests. You may want to make your lists separately and then merge your two lists. Remember, you are not yet evaluating the rules; you are simply trying to make a list of what you think the rules are. If the children are old enough, you might bring them into this process and let them help you make a list of "the rules in our house."

Look at each rule and ask: "Is this rule intentional? Is this a rule we have thought about, or is it simply a rule pulled from one of our childhoods or from some book we have read? Have we really taken time to discuss this rule? Is this a rule that we both agree has purpose? What are our children likely to learn from following this rule?"

Is it mutual? Have we both had input on this rule, or is it something one of us arbitrarily laid down years ago? If our children are old enough, have we brought them in to discuss the rule? Do they believe that it is a fair rule?

Is the rule reasonable? Does it serve a positive function? Remember the overarching question is: "Is this rule good for the child?"

The fourth area to examine in setting rules is: Have these rules been clearly understood by both the parents and the children? A rule that the parents have hidden in their minds but that has never been discussed openly with the children is not a rule the children can be expected to keep. When the parent disciplines a child for breaking such an unspoken rule, the child will feel that he or she has been unfairly treated.

WHAT ARE THE CONSEQUENCES?

The sign by the roadside said "$100 fine for littering." I took my candy wrapper and tucked it under the floor mat. I didn't have $100 I wanted to give to the city. The litter that lines our highways is testimony that consequences do not motivate everyone to obedience. Nor are consequences the only thing that motivates us to obedience. Having an aesthetic eye, I have always enjoyed driving down a highway uncluttered with cans, bags, and white pails. Therefore, my appreciation for beauty motivates me to hold on to my candy wrapper. But I must admit that an awareness of the $100 fine also adds to my motivation.

The breaking of civil rules usually brings negative consequences. One of the difficulties of our society is that, in recent years, the consequences of wrongdoing have been delayed by long and tedious court procedures, and on many occasions the consequences have been minimal. I believe that this has contributed to the growth of civil misconduct over the last several decades. Effective motivation to civil obedience requires quick and certain consequences.

In the family, the principle is the same. Obedience is learned by suffering the consequences of disobedience. Effective teaching of obedience requires that consequences for breaking rules should cause discomfort to the rule breaker. If the rule is that our children do not smoke cigarettes, then, if a child is caught smoking, he must immediately eat a carrot—the whole thing. This will give the body beta carotene to overcome the nicotine, and chances are he will think twice about smoking a second cigarette. If there is a second violation, a $25 donation to the American Heart Association, picking up a hundred cigarette butts from the street and putting them in the trash can, and reading an article on the dangers of nicotine to the lungs will probably be enough to convince him that smoking is for camels and not for children.

If a sixteen-year-old is found speeding, then he loses the privilege of driving for a week. A second offense would be loss of driving privileges for two weeks, and so forth. Not many teenagers would get beyond the two-week loss.

From these illustrations, perhaps you see the emerging pattern that consequences should be as closely associated to the rule as possible. It is especially helpful if the consequences for breaking basic family rules can be determined and discussed with the family at the time the rule is made. This has the advantage of the child's knowing ahead of time what the consequences will be, and it delivers the parent from the peril of having to make a snap judgment about what discipline should be applied. Deciding the consequences before the child breaks the rule is also more likely to give you a reasonable consequence.

As the children get older, you can let them be a part of deciding the consequences. Sometimes you will find that they are harder on themselves than you would be on them. My son suggested that if he did not bring his basketball home at the end of the day, then he should not be allowed to play basketball for two days. I would probably have chosen one day. But since he thought two days was a reasonable consequence, I agreed. When the children are a part of deciding the consequences before the rule is broken, they are far more likely to accept the consequence as being reasonable. This does not mean that the parent abdicates the final decision on what the consequence will be. If the child suggests a consequence that is not painful, then disobedience may be chosen more frequently because the consequences do not bring enough discomfort. Obedience is learned through suffering the consequences of misbehavior.

Sometimes, the consequence of disobedience on the part of a child will also make life more difficult for the parent. For example, when driving privileges are taken away from the sixteen-year-old, the parent must transport him to school and other activities, a chore that the parent so recently was happy to give up. But this is the nature of disobedience; it always affects others. A drunk driver does not simply hurt himself, but he is likely to destroy the property and sometimes the lives of others. One of the fundamental realities of life is that one's behavior affects others. The child seeing his mother suffering the consequences of his disobedience may be further motivated to obedience, assuming the child feels loved by the parents. Otherwise, such inconvenience or discomfort may be seen as deserved or as a way of getting back at the parent.

If you have never clearly delineated what the consequences will be, you have done whatever occurred to you at the moment and have likely found your spouse disagreeing with your discipline, at least sometimes. It is far easier to find agreement when you are not in the heat of the situation. Once you have agreed on the consequences, make sure that all family members understand what the consequences will be. This will make discipline much more acceptable to each child and will cause less conflict for parents. All of you are agreeing that if the rule is broken, these are the consequences. Whoever is at home administers the discipline, but it will be the same no matter which parent is the disciplinarian.

When a rule is broken and the parent is required to make sure that the child experiences the agreed-upon consequence, it is extremely helpful to give your child a dose of emotional love before and after the discipline. It is most helpful when you use the child's primary love language. For example, let's say that your son was playing football in the living room, a clear violation of rules. The agreed-upon discipline is that the football will be placed in the trunk of the car for two days, and thus the child would be unable to play football. If any item was broken by the football, the child must pay for the repair or replacement of the item with money out of his allowance.

Brian has clearly violated the rules, and in the process a vase was broken. The value of the vase is thirty dollars. Let's say that Brian's primary love language is words of affirmation. The parent may say something like this: "Brian, I think you know that I love you very much. Normally you follow the rules quite well. I am proud of you and your many accomplishments at school and at home. You make me a very happy parent. But when you break the rules, you know that you must suffer the consequences. One of the rules is that you will not play football in the living room. You know the rule, and you know the consequences. So let's go put the ball in the trunk and leave it there for the next two days. Also, you know that we agreed that you would pay for repairing or replacing any items that were broken. The vase cannot be repaired. To buy a new one will cost thirty dollars. So this will have to come out of your allowance over the next few weeks. I know that this will put pressure on you and you will not be able to do the things you would like to do with your money, but we all have to learn that when we disobey the rules, we have to suffer."

"But, Mom, Christmas is coming. I need my money to buy my gifts. I can't afford to lose thirty dollars," Brian protests.

"I understand that, son, and I know that it will be more difficult for you to buy gifts without the thirty dollars, but I also know that we agreed on the consequences of breaking the rules. I must be consistent in following what we agreed on. I just want you to know that I love you, and that's why I take the responsibility to help you learn to follow the rules." The parent may then reach out and give the child a hug. If both before and after affirming the consequences of the child's misbehavior, the parent expresses love in the child's primary love language, this is the most effective way to teach the child obedience. Even in suffering the consequences, he is assured of the parent's love.

Compare this to the common approach of the parent who hears the vase fall from the mantel, dashes to the living room, sees Brian picking up the football, and yells, "I have told you a thousand times—don't throw the football in the living room. Now look what you have done. You destroyed my vase. When are you ever going to learn? You act like a two-year-old kid. I don't know what I'm going to do with you. Get out of here." And the parent slaps Brian on the bottom as he leaves the room. Which of these two approaches is more likely to teach the child healthy obedience?

Now be honest. Which of these two approaches comes closer to the common approach you take when one of your children violates a rule? Which approach do you think is more productive? I think most parents will agree that the plan of clarifying the rule, agreeing on the consequences of misbehavior before it happens, and lovingly but firmly applying the consequences to the child is far more productive both for the child's learning and the parent's mental health.

WHEN CHILDREN MISBEHAVE...

Once the rules have been clearly defined and the consequences of misbehavior have been communicated to the child, it is the parents' responsibility to make sure that the child experiences the consequences of his misbehavior. When a parent is permissive one day and lets misbehavior slide, and the next day he comes down hard on the child for the same misbehavior, the parent is on the sure road of rearing a disobedient, disrespectful child. Inconsistent discipline is the most common pitfall of parents who are trying to raise responsible children. The consequences should be brought to bear as quickly after the disobedience has occurred as possible. Always, the discipline must be administered with love and firmness.

"But some days I am tired. I just don't feel like responding to my child's misbehavior." Welcome to the human race—all of us get tired. What parent has not been exasperated physically and emotionally from the pressures of life? But none of our resources are more important than our children. On these occasions, we must pull on our reserves and respond lovingly but firmly to our children's misbehavior.

Having the consequences for misbehavior set in advance keeps you from being controlled by your emotional state in the moment. If you have already agreed on what the consequences will be, your responsibility is simply to see that those consequences are carried out. You don't have to decide what will be done; you simply decide to follow through with what you have agreed would be done. You are not as likely to yell and scream or physically beat your children because of your own emotional state if you have already decided on the consequences.

Emily comes home in the afternoon. After a hug, a cookie, and a "How did your day go?" session, Mom says to her, "Emmy, you know the rule about your bed being made and your pajamas being put away before you leave for school in the morning. This morning your bed was unmade and your pajamas were on the floor. You know what we agreed on—that when you break the rule, there is no TV that night. Have a good time doing your homework, and then you may play games if you like, but there will be no TV tonight. I love you, and I know that you are going to learn to make your bed and put your pajamas away very soon."

"But, Mom, tonight is my very favorite show. All of my friends will be talking about it tomorrow, and I won't have any idea what they are talking about. Mom, please let me watch tonight. And then I won't watch it tomorrow night. Please, Mom, please."

Mom says, "I understand how much you want to watch TV tonight, but I also understand that you and I have agreed on the rules and what would be the consequences of your breaking the rules. I'm sorry, but you cannot watch it tonight." Mom remains kind and firm no matter what Emily's response, and Emily learns a big lesson that actions have consequences.

If Mom is consistent, loving, and kind but firm, she will have an efficient bed maker on her hands very shortly. If, on the other hand, Mom is inconsistent, gives in, or doesn't see that Emmy suffers the consequences of her misbehavior, Mom may be making beds and picking up pajamas when her daughter is fifteen. The above illustration reveals the steps in administering discipline: (1) We make sure we express love and care for the child. This was done by hugging, giving a cookie, and having conversation about today's events. (2) We affirm clearly that a rule has been broken. We remind the child of the consequences we have agreed on. (3) Then we make certain that the child experiences the consequences. We listen to the child's rebuttal, but kindly and firmly we assure the child that he or she must suffer the consequences of wrongdoing or negligence.

Sometimes, this is very painful for the parent. For example, Mom and Alex have agreed that if Alex does not complete his homework, he will not go to ball practice the next afternoon. One evening Alex fails to do his homework and Dad informs him that he will not be able to go to practice the next afternoon. "But, Dad, the big game is Saturday. If I don't go to practice tomorrow, I won't get to play in the game. Dad, I've been waiting for this for a long time. Dad, please don't do this to me."

"Son, I'm not doing anything to you. You did it to yourself. You knew the rule about homework. You had plenty of time to do your homework. You chose rather to watch TV and play games with Michael. Now, I am sorry, but we agreed on the rule, and we agreed on the consequences."

"But, Dad, you know how much this means to me. Let me miss practice next week, but not tomorrow. Not tomorrow, Dad." What's a father to do? The answer is simple but not easy. Be kind, be loving, but be firm. Missing the big game will not destroy your child's chance at a college scholarship five years later, but missing the big game will teach your child that there are always painful results when we disobey the rules. It is this reality that motivates children to obedience.

Such discipline must always be done in a spirit of love with the parent in full control of his or her emotions, never accompanied with screaming and yelling, but always accompanied with deep sympathy for the child's pain. The child should realize that we, too, suffer because he will not be able to play in the big game, but that is the reality of life. When one person disobeys, others inevitably suffer. It is through his or her suffering that the child learns obedience, and through consistency that the parent earns the right to be honored.

CHAPTER NINE

The Gift of Honor

It was a cold winter day, and the issues I had dealt with had been extremely stressful. All of that seemed to evaporate when I walked into my office and found the following handwritten note from my nine-year-old daughter.

Dear Dad,

I love you very much. I know that you work hard and help a lot of people. I appreciate all the things you do for me. I'm glad that you are my father.

Love,
Shelley

Not only did the words give me warm emotions, but I knew that she was learning to show honor. I read the note around the dinner table for the whole family, including John. Surely he could see from my smile and the moisture gathering in my eyes that this was the gravy part of being a parent. This was payday! This was the reward of toil. When a child begins to recognize and appreciate the effort you have put forth in being a parent, all of the dirty diapers, trips to the doctor, sleepless nights, and the hard work of loving discipline somehow seem like a good investment.

Please notice that the chapter on obedience precedes the chapter on honor. That is the chronological order. Toddlers are not capable of honoring parents; their world still revolves around their own ego. I do not mean that they are unaware of the presence of parents, but the focus of their minds is on getting their own needs met and exploring their own desires. They are fully capable of learning obedience, but the capacity to honor comes much later in childhood.

Honor is the expression of respect or esteem. It is recognizing the importance of someone and seeking to express love and devotion to that person. To honor someone is to draw attention to that person's character. In order to truly honor parents, a child must come to understand something of the nature of right and wrong, of sacrifice and love. The desire to honor comes from recognizing that parents have made right decisions and have sacrificially loved the child and each other. A child comes to respect and honor a parent when he recognizes that the parent's behavior has been truly good.

I must pause long enough to say that there is an honor, however diluted, that honors parents for position and not character. The parents have given the child life; therefore, they are exceedingly important. The child honors them for the importance of their position as parents but acknowledges that, when their character is observed, the parents are not worthy of honor. Tragically, many children in our generation, if they are to express honor at all, must express it on this shallow level. But this is not the characteristic of a functional family.

A deeper, true honor is always earned. Let me illustrate. It is hard to imagine that the son of a slave would be offered a job at $100,000 a year. It is even more incredible that the same man would turn down the offer, but that is exactly what George Washington Carver did. The offer was made by inventor Thomas Edison. Henry Ford also tried to persuade Carver to work for the Ford Motor Company, but Carver was unimpressed with the offers of money and prestige. He chose rather to live in the South, living in relative poverty, wearing the same suit for forty years. He had earlier given up a promising position at Iowa State University in order to work with Booker T. Washington in his struggling Tuskegee Institute. When friends argued that he could help his people if he had all that money, Carver replied, "If I had all that money, I might forget about my people." On his tombstone are carved the following words: "He could have added fortune to fame, but caring for neither, he found happiness and honor in being helpful to the world."[1] People still honor George Washington Carver. Why? Because he lived a self-sacrificing life for the benefit of others. True honor is always earned.

Sometimes earning honor is hard work. Our children see our weaknesses and irritating habits, and they see the selfish part of our nature far better than we suspect. It is just as important for us to keep a wall from being built in this relationship as in the relationship with our spouse. When Derek was fifteen, he and I had a discussion in which some unkind words were exchanged. He walked out of the house, and I sat down. My first thoughts were on the injustice of his words to me. But my conscience got hold of me, and I realized some of my own words had been less than honorable. I had blown it. I prayed and asked God to forgive me, and I knew I needed to find my son and ask his forgiveness as well.

Before I could leave to find him, Derek walked back into the house.

"Son, I'm sorry. Will you forgive me?" I asked.

"Dad, I'm the one who was wrong. I shouldn't have said what I did." We forgave each other, and I rejoiced that he had learned both the humility of asking for forgiveness and the grace and honor of forgiving.

"YOU AND DADDY DID A REALLY GOOD JOB"

The capacity for honor is only slightly developed in the early childhood years. It reaches its finest hour three or four years after the child has grown up. I know one woman whose daughter, now in her early twenties and newly married, told her not long ago, "You and Daddy did a really good job raising me." The mother, who, like all parents, sometimes questioned how "well" she and her husband did as parents, became misty-eyed and gave her daughter a big hug. "You made it easy, kiddo," she said.

But honor can be cultivated in younger children as well. If a child has been taught to stand when an adult enters a room, it is at first a perfunctory act. But in due time, it may become an expression of genuine honor. If the child is instructed not to interrupt a parent who is talking, it will at first be simply a learned behavior, but in due time, it may become an expression of honor, recognizing the worth of another individual and the disrespect shown when one is interrupted. Offering help when help is needed can be an expression of honor to parents. When a twelve-year-old offers to wash dishes when it is not "his turn," it may be an expression of honor. (It may also be an expression of manipulation, an effort to get the parents to buy the expensive tennis shoes that they have been reluctant to buy.) True honor is a matter of the heart, not a particular action. But genuine honor is expressed by means of common courtesies to the parent.

A second way children express honor to parents is by words of appreciation. "Mommy, that was a good dinner" may be simply a polite gesture that gets the child a smile from the mother, but such a statement may also be an expression of awareness of the value of their mother's time and expertise in meal preparation. "Thanks for coming to the game, Dad" may be simply a desire: "I wish you would come to all of my games." But it may also be an honest recognition of the effort Dad had to make to attend the game.

If spoken words of appreciation express honor, written words may be even more powerful. Imagine how I felt when I read the following classroom assignment written by my son, Derek, when he was in the third grade. The assignment was to write an article describing himself.

MYSELF
by Derek C.

Well, I really enjoy football. I enjoy playing and watching football. I also enjoy basketball. I guess I am pretty good in both of them! I have a family of four not counting my dog, Zacchaeus. We call him Zac for short. He's half dachshund and half poodle. He's very short and doesn't grow. I like some girls. I have a bunch of friends. Some people know me and I don't know them. Like sometimes, people come up and say "Hey, Derek." I say "Hey" and don't know them. Well, I also lift weights and work out by playing sports! Well, that's about all I can think of now so that's it, except for me and my father are good friends and we play with each other. By Derek Chapman. The End.

I made it fine until I came to the last two lines, then the tears began to flow. It was not written as an expression of honor to me but rather as a classroom assignment. But I knew that honor was in his heart, and somehow it made all the hours invested with him worthwhile.

MOM

To what flashes in lightning
and rushes me to rivers
To an open mouth full of song
calling out into the storm of faces—
You are surrounded in Song

To exploding corners
and laughing hallways
and yellow kitchens
bathed in butterflies

To tea time and pastries,
lace and fresh flowers,
gardens and bird baths,
chocolates and popcorn

To embracing the pastry of life with blooming arms
and to singing
a new song
every day . . .

To Mother

DAD

To what waits in silence
To what hears hearts
To what grasps gently
To what climbs without clamor
To what listens with care
To what cares most

To what in me that is you, Father

Derek Chapman

As children mature into adulthood and parents enter old age, if honor is in the heart of adult children, it will be expressed by visits, phone calls, cards, and caring for physical needs. Every time I visit my aging parents, I am reminded that I am modeling honor for my own children. Our daughter, Shelley, is now a physician, and our son is a writer. Knowing the meager income of most writers, Derek is already looking to the future. He said recently to his mother, "Don't worry, Mom. If anything happens to Dad, I'll make sure that Shelley puts you in a nice nursing home and I will come to visit you regularly."

Ultimately, children honor parents by the way they invest their lives. The saddest of all parents are those whose children have chosen drugs, alcohol, crime, or other irresponsible lifestyles. The happiest of parents are those who are honored by children who choose a self-giving lifestyle, investing life for the benefit of God and good in the world. These are above all parents most honored.

For more information on how you can teach your children to honor and respect others, see the code on page 177 to access the Family Adventure Guide at **www.5lovelanguages .com/5traits**. This guide is to help put into practice the healthy traits discussed in this book. You'll find a number of assessments, things to think about, and opportunities for deeper discussion.

PART FIVE

Husbands Who Love and Lead

CHAPTER TEN

The Meaning of "Leading"

For many contemporary wives, the idea of a husband as "leader" is confusing and controversial. Some husbands have abused this idea and run their families with an iron fist. But I've observed that the greater danger is the passive, uninvolved husband who "outsources" all the family-related activities and decisions to his wife.

Somewhere between these two extremes is a healthy middle road where the husband is responsible, dependable, and deeply committed to his wife and family. He is able to express both pain and joy, sympathy and encouragement. He is able to relate to his wife on an emotional level. On the other hand, he is strong and dependable, feeling a sense of responsibility for the well-being of his wife and family. He does not run when things get tough but looks for solutions that will benefit the whole family. He is a leader to be sure, but he does not lead in isolation. He recognizes that the most effective leaders are servants, not dictators. He values the partnership with his wife; he wants to be there for her, but he has no desire to dominate her. This is the husband in a functional family.

"I FEEL LIKE I HAVE THREE CHILDREN INSTEAD OF TWO"

Elaine had been married for ten years. She was in my office alone, although her husband had come with her for several counseling appointments. This time, she said, "He was ashamed to come. He lost his job last week because he got in a fight with a fellow employee." This had been his pattern for ten years. The longest time he had held a job was eighteen months. He didn't always get into a fight, but he did always get frustrated with the job or the people with whom he worked.

His normal pattern was simply to walk off the job with no explanation and fade away. The employer typically called Elaine to ask what the problem was and if he was coming back. She would explain that he had told her that he had quit his job; therefore, she assumed that he would not be returning. He would go weeks and sometimes months without work, spending his time sleeping late, watching TV, and working out at the local gym. Elaine had worked a full-time job all ten years of their marriage except for brief times surrounding the births of their two children. When her husband was working, he helped her with the bills, but when he was out of work, she had to carry the whole load.

With the tears flowing freely, Elaine said, "I don't know how much longer I can go on. I feel like I have three children instead of two. Not only does he give up jobs because things don't go his way, he also must have his way about everything. He won't give up an hour at the gym to stay with the children while I go for a doctor's appointment. I have to drop the children off at my mother's so as not to interrupt his schedule. I am totally exasperated. I have never had a real husband."

Tracy has a very different problem with her husband. "Dr. Chapman, I don't understand why he must control everything. I can't even sneeze without running into another room because he doesn't want me to sneeze in his presence. He is a hardworking man, and he makes good money. He pays all the bills. I have no complaints about the way he provides financially, but he treats me like my ideas are worth nothing, like I'm a child rather than his wife. He won't even let me see the checkbook, and if I ask him any questions about our financial situation, he gets angry. It's like he runs everything, and I'm just along for the ride. I have a hard time responding to him sexually because I feel like he treats me as a nonperson. I know this is not the way a marriage should be, but I don't know what to do."

Then there is Becky. Becky has been married for fifteen years. She and her husband both work full-time. They have three children. Her complaint has nothing to do with finances. She is, however, extremely distressed over her husband's passive lifestyle. "He takes no initiative to do anything except to go to work regularly. Our bedroom has needed painting for six years. Over and over again he says, 'I'll get around to it,' but he never has. The children's bicycles stay broken for months before he finally gets around to fixing them. Our money sits in a passbook savings account and he will take no initiative to try to discover an investment where we can get a better return. In the summer, the grass gets mowed every three weeks. I am ashamed to have my friends come by. In fact, last summer, I finally hired someone to mow the grass every week. He spends his time with his computer. Everyone talks about how great computers are. Actually, I hate them. I wish the thing would just explode and he would wake up to the real world. I've tried everything I know. I've tried calmly discussing the matter with him. I've tried screaming at him. I've tried ignoring the problem. I've tried being overly kind to him. Nothing seems to make a difference. I don't know what else to do."

Three wives—all in very different situations, but all desperately crying for loving leadership on the part of their husbands. Volumes could be written simply telling similar stories of wives who live with constant pain and disappointment. The husbands of Elaine, Tracy, and Becky are different from one another. Some of their problems reveal basic immaturity, lack of responsibility, and poor character development. Some exhibit controlling personalities, and all of them show poor relationship skills. These basic issues will need to be addressed if they are to be loving leaders.

However, for other husbands, the problem is not that they are unwilling or unable to be leaders in the marriage. The problem is that many men do not know how. They have no visual image; they have no concrete ideas of how the role of the husband as loving leader is to be played out in daily life. They are limited only to the example of their own fathers and to the ideas they pick up from media or other guys.

A LOOK AT THE HEALTHY HUSBAND

What does a healthy husband look like? What steps can I take to stimulate growth and health in my role (or my spouse's role) as a husband? Here are some guidelines.

1. *A loving husband views his wife as a partner.* A wife is not a trophy to be won in courtship and then placed on the wall for all to observe along with our ten-point buck. She is a living person with whom to have a relationship. She is not a person to be dominated and controlled to satisfy our own goals. She is a person to be known who has goals of her own. She is not a child to be patronized. She is a partner with whom her husband is developing a relationship.

The idea of the wife as partner is as old as creation. Note in Genesis that while God instructs the man and woman to subdue the earth and rule over the fish of the sea, the birds of the air, and other living creatures, the man is told to become "one flesh" with his wife, not to dominate her.

Partnership is to permeate the entire marriage. Let me apply this concept to the area of decision making. When the husband truly views his wife as a partner, he will want decision making to be a joint experience. Perhaps in a given area, he will have more knowledge than she does. In another area, she may have more knowledge than he does. Seldom do we have the same amount of information regarding a given topic; so when we make decisions together, each gets the benefit of the knowledge and information the other has experienced or gleaned through the years. Partnership means that our goal is to make the best possible decision. Our personality type may be a "controller" or we may be "passive," but we do not wish to allow our personality tendencies to dictate our decision-making process. We are consciously exalting partnership as being more important than our personality traits.

The husband as lover will be thinking about what is best for his wife, and his emphasis will be upon guiding the decision in that direction. If the wife is also loving, her focus will be on what is best for the husband. Ideally, after discussion of an issue a decision or compromise will be clear. Even when it is not, decision making will not be a game of manipulation where each is trying to get his own way. It will, in fact, be a partnership where each is looking out for the benefit of the other, and the result is a decision that is best for the whole or best for both of them.

As a leader, the husband takes the initiative in creating an atmosphere where this partnership can be played out without undue tension. He assures his wife that he sees her as a partner and deeply desires her input on the decision. When a child expresses desires, the father evaluates them and makes the final decision as to what is best for the child. The husband does not take his wife's input that way. He sees her as an equal partner and has no desire to dominate her in the decision-making process. Nor will the loving leader be a dictator who makes decisions independently of his wife and informs her after the fact. This often happens in the business world where management makes the decisions and informs employees. But in marriage, both husband and wife are in management of the home. The loving leader recognizes this and seeks to create an emotional climate where free interchange of ideas can be done without a spirit of domination or intimidation.

On the other hand, the loving leader will not abandon the decision-making process and simply throw the ball to his wife. The "do what you want to do" attitude is not taking the leadership in partnership. Sometimes this attitude develops with the husband who has difficulty making decisions and finds it easier to yield that responsibility to the wife. Other times, this attitude develops out of a sense of resentment that the wife is going to have her way no matter what, so why fight it; just give up. Whatever the source of the attitude, it is not the position of the loving leader. The loving husband who finds this attitude arising within will seek to analyze the source and deal with it in a responsible manner so that he can return to the practice of partnership in decision making.

We are also partners in the financial area of marriage. Being partners does not mean that we do the same thing. In fact, in a true partnership, almost never do we each perform the same function. There are many models of financial partnership in a marriage. One is not necessarily better than another. Each couple must forge the model that fits the husband and wife's personality, talents, desires, and values.

For Bob, the model is very simple. "I make the money; she spends the money. It's a good arrangement. It works for us, and we're both happy with it." Another young couple are both medical doctors. "We both work; neither of us has time to spend the money; therefore, we have become wealthy. So far, so good. I don't know what will happen when one or both of us stop working."

Most models are not as extreme as these two illustrations, but there is no perfect financial model. What is important is that both of you have a sense of partnership in family finances. One of you may "keep the books," or you may choose to do it together. What is best in your marriage is what the two of you agree on as partners. If either of you feels dominated or deserted, then you are not experiencing partnership. You may come to the financial table with different ideas, desires, and values. The loving husband takes the lead in seeing that these differences are fairly negotiated. If he must "tip the scale," he does so in the direction of what is best for his wife. He is a loving leader with emphasis on loving.

2. *A loving husband will communicate with his wife.* As I've explored in detail in my book *The Marriage You've Always Wanted*, many, though not all, men are much less verbally communicative than women. Therefore, many husbands will have to push themselves to go beyond what is "natural" for them in order to meet their wives' need for communication.

Life is shared primarily by means of communication, particularly discussing our thoughts, feelings, and desires. These cannot be observed in our behavior. A wife may guess what is going on in her husband's mind by his behavior, but unless that behavior is a pattern that he has exhibited with certain thoughts and desires previously, she is not likely to guess correctly. The old saying "I can read him like a book" is only true after there have been years of vigorous communication, and even then, it is only true in a limited sense. One of a wife's deepest desires is to know her husband. When he talks about his thoughts, feelings, and desires she feels that he is allowing her into his life. When a husband goes long periods without talking about what he is feeling, she has the sense that he is cutting her out, and she feels isolated.

Sometimes a wife stifles her husband's communication by her argumentative spirit or judgmental responses. Some time ago a husband said to me, "Dr. Chapman, I've just stopped sharing my thoughts with my wife because every time I discuss a thought with her, she pounces on it. She either disagrees with it or questions me about it or gives me a different perspective. It's as though I'm not allowed to have a thought that she doesn't want to scrutinize. I would be happy to tell my thoughts if she'd simply accept them as my thoughts." After two counseling sessions, it became obvious that part of the problem was his own defensiveness. Having had his ideas put down as a child, he had subconsciously determined that as an adult, his ideas would always be right; thus, he became defensive whenever his wife or anyone else questioned his ideas.

Part of the problem also lay in his wife's obsession with evaluating ideas and discussing each one to the final conclusion, proving one to be right and the other to be wrong. This pattern of communication is very stifling. Either of these patterns typically takes the help of a counselor to bring the couple to understand what is going on and to change the patterns. Whatever stops the flow of your communication needs to be discovered and eliminated. If you can do this by discussion between the two of you, fine. If not, then it is advisable to discuss it with a friend or to go for professional counseling.

We cannot afford to let communication come to a halt or to allow communication to simply be the battlefield upon which we fight out our differences. Positive, open, free, accepting communication is the characteristic of a functional marriage. The husband as loving leader must take the initiative in seeing that this kind of communication becomes a way of life.

3. *A loving husband will put his wife at the top of his priority list.* All of us live by priorities. We may never have written a list of our priorities, but in our minds we rank some things as more important than others. These priorities are revealed most often by our actions. Answer the questions, "How do I spend my time? How do I invest my money? How do I use my energy?" and you will have the answer to the question, "What are my priorities?"

Many things compete for our attention in a marriage—work, chores, children, other outside commitments, perhaps our own parents' needs. Let me address children in particular. A husband can be critical of his wife after the children come; he may feel that the children have "replaced" him in his wife's eyes. This is a legitimate concern—and in fact is often the case. But it may also be true of the husband, particularly in a marriage where his emotional needs are not adequately met by the wife or he feels somewhat estranged from her. He may find himself focusing more time and energy on the children because he is receiving more feedback from them. The loving leader, if he observes this in his own behavior, will recognize this as unhealthy and will take steps to refocus his time and energy toward meeting the needs of his wife and helping her learn how in turn to meet his needs.

4. *A loving husband will love his wife unconditionally.* Unconditional love means that we love the individual and thus seek her best interest *regardless* of her response to us. This is profoundly countercultural. Contemporary ideas of love run along the lines of "I will love you if you will love me." We tend to be egocentric even in marriage. The focus of our effort is to get our own needs met. In fact, much of modern psychology has emphasized this as normal behavior. Some have gone so far as to say that all of our behavior toward others is motivated by getting our own needs met.

Unconditional love, on the other hand, focuses on meeting the needs of the other person. In marriage, it is the husband looking out for the wife's best interest. It is supporting her in her endeavors even when he may not totally agree with them. It is helping her reach her goals and aspirations because he values her as a person. It is not "I'll put the kids to bed if you will give me sex." It is "I'll put the kids to bed because I know you are tired."

All of us would like to think that someone loves us unconditionally. The child longs for this kind of love from his parents, but husbands and wives also desire unconditional love from each other. The wedding vow was to love "in sickness and in health, in poverty and in wealth, so long as we both shall live." This is a commitment to unconditional love. In a healthy marriage, we will actually experience it.

Far too many husbands who view themselves as macho leaders are waiting for their wives to take the lead in unconditional love. They are sitting back saying, "When she decides to become affectionate, when she decides to think about *my* needs, when she decides to be more responsive to me, then I'll start loving her." But a healthy husband will take the lead in unconditional love. Since this need is so fundamental to one's emotional health, most wives will respond positively to a husband who loves them unconditionally. Far too many wives live with a haunting feeling that unless they perform sexually or otherwise in an approved manner, their husbands' love will be withdrawn. This does not engender a healthy marriage.

5. *A loving husband is committed to discovering and meeting his wife's needs.* Perhaps this seems redundant in the light of what we have just said about unconditional love. But it has been my observation through the years that many husbands simply do not understand the needs of their wives. Consequently, in their ignorance, they make no effort to meet those needs. Some husbands believe that if they work at a steady job and bring home a decent salary, they have completed their role as husband. But a wife's most basic emotional need is to feel cared for. The functional husband will discover his wife's primary love language and will speak it regularly while sprinkling in the other four. His wife will live with a full love tank, and chances are she will greatly admire and respond to the husband who is meeting this need.

Her need for security is also fundamental. It is first a physical need—what husband hasn't stumbled out of bed at three in the morning to investigate a "strange sound"?—but her greatest security need is the need for the deep assurance that her husband is committed to her. The husband who threatens his wife with words of divorce or offhandedly makes comments like "You'd be better off with somebody else" or "I think I'll find someone else" is playing into a harmful pattern. The loving husband will make every effort to communicate to his wife that whatever happens, he is with her. If there are disagreements, he will take the time to listen, understand, and seek resolution. If she suffers physical or emotional pain, he will be by her side. Betsy expressed it well when she said about her husband, "I know that Greg is with me no matter what happens. He is committed to our marriage. It gives me such a feeling of security."

The loving husband is also concerned about his wife's sense of self-worth. If she finds fulfillment and meaning from playing softball, then he will be her number one cheerleader. If she finds fulfillment in being the best computer expert with the company, he is there to express his admiration for her skills. If she chooses to be a "work at home" mother, he will support her decision wholeheartedly. Any of these avenues of gaining self-worth may cause him some emotional concern or require more physical work on his part. But he is willing to talk with her about his emotional struggles and seek understanding and unity because he is committed to her well-being.

We are not only physical and emotional, but we are also social creatures. Some men resist their wives' need to develop social relationships outside job and family, or at least passively let their wives plan all their social commitments. A wife may want her husband to attend the symphony with her. She may want him to initiate a neighborhood dinner or participate with her in a church Bible study. Such activities may not be on the top of his priority list, but they quickly ascend in importance because meeting her needs is important to him. He recognizes that in helping her develop social relationships, he is enhancing her sense of fulfillment. He does not decry these things or put them down as being superficial and unimportant. He sees them as a normal part of her life, and he allows her interests to lead him to meet her needs.

6. *A loving husband will seek to model his spiritual and moral values.* All men have spiritual and moral values. By moral values, I mean a set of beliefs about what is right and wrong. By spiritual values, I mean a set of beliefs about what exists beyond the material world.

In a healthy, loving family, what a man values will be shown by how he lives. The closer a man comes to living by worthy spiritual and moral beliefs, the more he will be respected by his wife. The greater the gap between what he proclaims to believe on these issues and what he actually does, the greater the disrespect he engenders.

It is true that some men are not as comfortable with open, verbal displays of spiritual commitment as women are, or may express their faith commitment in other ways—for example, serving alongside other men in a church work project. Therefore, it is important to look beyond specific practices such as "leads family devotions" to such broad areas as kindness, integrity, and dependability.

In spiritual and moral issues, the husband's best leadership tool is his own model. If the wife sees his life as being consistent with what he says he believes, she will respect him even if she disagrees with his beliefs. But if he does not live by his espoused beliefs, then she loses her respect for him. This does not mean that the husband must be perfect. It does mean that he must make a conscientious effort to apply his spiritual and moral beliefs to his own lifestyle. When he fails, he must be willing to acknowledge his failure and ask forgiveness. It is in this act of confession that he demonstrates that his beliefs are strong and genuine and that he will not excuse himself for wrong behavior. Spiritual and moral beliefs are better caught than taught. The loving husband will seek diligently to be authentic. Such authenticity will have a positive influence upon his wife and his children. Anything less will make him appear hypocritical.

Before leaving this area, I must acknowledge that within the Christian worldview, such authentic living is not thought to be obtained by human effort but is the result of a person's opening his life to the Spirit of Christ and allowing that Spirit to shape his thinking and actions. It is a cooperative effort between his spirit and the Spirit of God. It is not the result of isolated self-discipline. This, in fact, is one of the unique distinctions of the Christian faith. It is a reality that personally I have found to be extremely liberating.

While not a comprehensive list, the six characteristics listed above will serve as guidelines for the husband who seeks to be a loving leader in his marriage. I wish that in the early days of my marriage someone had given me such a list. Most of the above principles I learned through several years of intense marital struggles. Most of these characteristics were not true in the early years of my own marriage. In my mind, that accounts for most of the difficulties my wife and I encountered in those years. By the time John, our live-in anthropologist, spent the year with us, most of these characteristics had been developed to some degree in my relationship with Karolyn. Here in John's own words is what he observed.

I saw you as the spiritual leader in the home. You took initiative in such things as reading the Bible with the family and prayers at meals, but I never felt you did this in a domineering way. It seemed like a natural part of life. The whole family was involved.

I remember you seemed eager to serve Karolyn. You seemed to respect her greatly. I never felt you took advantage of her. You viewed her as an equal partner. Actually both of you showed genuine respect for each other. You were very different in personality, but you seemed to complement each other. Neither seemed to be jealous of the other. You worked well as a team. I'm still in admiration of that.

CHAPTER ELEVEN

What Fathers Do for Their Families

In my own counseling, I often have encountered people struggling with what has been called "father hunger." In my opinion much of the anger, depression, and confusion that I observe in the lives of young adults is rooted in a hunger for a father connection. This father hunger results from receiving too little quantity and quality of fathering as a child, too little intimacy between father and child.

It seems to me that this father deficiency comes from three categories of fathers. First, and most obvious, is the absentee father. Death, divorce, and desertion have left millions of children without fathers. Roughly 23 percent of children growing up in the US will spend a portion of their lives before the age of eighteen in a single-parent home, and most of these children will have minimal contact with their fathers.[1]

The second category is what I call the "present but not available" father. This is the father who lives in the same house with the child and mother but has little time available for fathering. The salesman who is gone all week and is exhausted on the weekends or the executive who spends fourteen hours a day commuting and working and only sees the child when the child is asleep are examples of this category. The third category is helpless fathers. They live in the home but have no idea how to build an intimate relationship with their children. They don't know how to father because they were never fathered.

Unfortunately, some of these fathers received harsh treatment from their fathers and now duplicate that with their own children. Children who grow up in these homes not only suffer from father deficiency, but often are filled with intense anger at their fathers, which expresses itself in various antisocial behaviors. These fathers destroy rather than build their children. The father who beats, molests, verbally denounces, or disrupts the stability of the home by his alcohol, gambling, drugs, or extreme moodiness is, in effect, an antifather. He steals the carefree laughter of childhood.

It is my deeply held opinion that if the fathers in these three categories could become loving leaders to their children, we could radically change the social landscape of the next generation. We would keep millions of children from self-destructing, and we would see our communities filled with children laughing, playing, and learning; developing their creative and intellectual potentials and becoming responsible, caring adults. Some would say it is an impossible dream, but it is nevertheless my constant vision. It is what motivates me to lead seminars and workshops and to invest hours in the counseling office, helping fathers see the importance of their role in healthy fathering and learning how to do it effectively.

It is not my purpose in this chapter to minimize the role of the mother in nurturing the child. That role is absolutely essential to a healthy child, but it is my observation that the mothers of this generation are doing a far better job than the fathers. A part of this is because until quite recently, fathers have not been taught the extreme importance of the father-child relationship. I like the way Schaller puts it: "A child's father is typically the first male to write his thoughts and feelings on his child's heart."[2]

WHAT OUR FATHERS GIVE US

Much of the child's self-identity will be influenced by the father's words and treatment. The child will come to believe that he is special, valuable, good, or a worthless brat largely from the messages he receives from his father. I saw this graphically illustrated in my office by Pam, who said, "I never felt that I was as smart as other people. I've always felt that other people have more abilities than I." In fact, she was an extremely successful accountant; her peers admired her accomplishments. It became apparent in further conversation that what Pam felt was directly related to the messages she had heard from her father in childhood. As Dr. Schaller puts it, "Our fathers are carried around inside us long after they have died. We continue to model them, dialogue with them, and listen to them. . . . Many of us continue to mirror the image of ourselves that our fathers have written on our souls."[3] Adults who did not receive a positive self-image from their fathers when they were children may feel insecure for a lifetime. Those who did receive positive, supportive messages from their dads will usually be strong even in the midst of adversity.

A father also strongly influences a child's level of motivation. When our daughter graduated from medical school, the copresident of the graduating class, Karen Popovich, addressed the audience. I was deeply moved when I heard that her father, also a physician, had died a month earlier. With quiet confidence, she addressed the audience, acknowledging that her father's death had reminded her that medical science has limitations. But reflecting on her own accomplishments, she honored her father when she said, "My accomplishments are to a large degree a tribute to my father who taught me through the years that we can accomplish whatever we dream. He instilled in me a positive spirit to accomplish all that I was capable of accomplishing. I shall always be indebted to him." With gracious words, she demonstrated the influence of a father on a child's level of motivation.

The child's sexual identity is also strongly influenced by the father-child relationship. In a functional family, the father recognizes that his role is as important as that of the mother in nurturing the femininity of his daughter and the masculinity of his son. Regular expressions of love, strong supportive words, and recognition of her accomplishments go a long way in helping his daughter become a secure, loving, joyful woman. Such words and actions are no less important to the son's developing masculinity. This does not mean forcing the son into your own ideas of what it means to be male; it does mean encouraging him in his own interests and letting him know that whatever his interests, you are there to support and encourage him. Studies have shown the importance of a strong father connection in the child's developing sexuality.

Another area in which the father influences the child is in the child's pattern of relating to other people. What fathers communicate and demonstrate about relationships strongly influences the way in which their children relate to people. If the father communicates to a son that men do not talk about feelings, his son will likely have great difficulty in discussing his feelings with his future wife. If a father indicates that people cannot be trusted, his children will have greater difficulty developing trust in relationships.

If, on the other hand, the father communicates that nothing is more important in life than relationships, if the use of his time and money shows that he really believes this, then his children will likely grow up to be people who put relationships high on their list of priorities. If fathers demonstrate that anger is to be acknowledged but controlled, that we are to process our anger without violence, the child will be far more likely to view anger as a healthy emotion and learn ways to process anger constructively. The father's role in teaching children relationship skills is extremely important.

CHARACTERISTICS OF A LOVING FATHER

1. *A loving father will be actively involved.* The father will take the lead, the initiative. In his role as father, he will aggressively seek to be involved in the child's life from the very beginning. The passive father is a responder. He relates to the child only when the child initiates the process. When the child cries and later begs or pulls, the passive father responds. In a healthy family, the father is always looking for ways to be involved in his children's lives. He does not wait for their call but anticipates how he might stimulate their minds or emotions to positive growth.

One of my personal regrets is that both of our children were born in the old medical regime that did not allow the father into the delivery room. It seems to me that the current practice of encouraging fathers to participate in the birth of their children is a far healthier beginning toward a life of active fathering.

Though I was not allowed in the delivery room, I learned early to be an active father. I cherish the memories of holding my children as infants, moving my head back and forth to see if their eyes followed, talking "baby talk" (which in any other context would make a man appear insane). A few months later I lay on the floor and let the children crawl over me and hit me with stuffed bears. (It is always important what you allow in the hands of small children. They will either eat it or use it as a weapon against you.) Then came balls, trucks, and tricycles. I got into all of them. This is the joy of parenting—you can regress and not lose your status.

2. *A loving father will make time to be with his children.* I emphasize "make time," because the demands of today's business and professional world, and the long commutes many of us face, make involved parenting even more difficult. But even dads who stay closer to home can be "absentee" fathers, spending long hours at the computer, for example. Mothers who work outside the home have

had to learn to juggle and sacrifice to make time for their children. Dads can do the same.

One of the things that John observed while living in our home for a year is that when I had evening responsibilities, I would arrange my schedule so that I could come home in the afternoon near the time when the children arrived home from school and spend a couple of hours helping them with homework or playing with them. He saw me taking each of the children out to breakfast once a month simply to have quality time with them individually. Had he been there a few years later, he would have seen me adjusting my schedule to attend Little League football games and, later still, high school basketball games where Derek was playing. He would have seen me working my schedule to attend piano recitals and other musical events in which our daughter was involved. He would have seen me taking walks with my daughter two or three evenings a week to talk about books, boys, and other important subjects. He would have seen me propping my eyes open to have in-depth conversations with my son, whose intellectual and emotional motors seem to come on after 11:00 p.m. It was not easy to make time for fathering, but I am grateful that early on, I learned something of the importance of fathering. Today, our father-child connection is still strong.

3. *A loving father engages his children in conversation.* "What happened at school today?" Mark asked his fourth-grade daughter, Katie.

"I got an A in art," she said.

"Wonderful," Mark responded. "May I see it?"

"Sure," she said as she laid it on the table.

"I like it. Tell me, what was going on in your mind as you were painting this picture?"

"Well, when I was painting the sky, I was thinking about our time at the beach this summer. Remember when the sky was so blue and we lay on the sand and looked up at the clouds?"

"I remember," said Mark. "The sand was so warm."

"Except when the waves came," Katie reminded him.

"Yes, and we both got wet," Mark said. "What do you like most about going to the beach?" he asked.

"I think the sky. It's always so beautiful, and at night you can see the stars. It's not like in the city. The stars are so bright."

"Remember the night we saw the Big Dipper?" Mark asked.

"Yes," said Katie, "and Sam never could find it."

Mark laughed and said, "But he will. Maybe next year. So what else were you thinking about when you drew the picture?"

And so the conversation goes. And so, the father connection is developed.

There is no substitute for regular conversation. It is the vehicle whereby the father and child discuss thoughts, feelings, ideas, desires, and decisions. It is where a child learns of a father's history and a father teaches his values. It is where a child asks questions and receives answers, where a father gives encouragement and plants ideas.

4. *A loving father plays with his children.* This can be the fun part of fathering—unless, of course, you have the distorted idea that play is for children and work is for parents. In reality, play affords us the opportunity of entering into our child's world at each level of development. For the child in the crib, we are waving bright objects and watching his eyes move from side to side. We are placing objects a few inches away and watching the child stretch and bring the object to his mouth. Later, we are rolling balls and reading storybooks. Still later, we are throwing footballs and playing on the computer. But all the while, we are sharing life with our children.

A common problem is that fathers often want to make play into work. Their emphasis is on winning and "doing it right" rather than having fun. I've known fathers who would never let their child win at any game. Their philosophy was that if they demonstrated a higher level of proficiency, the child would be motivated to beat them and thus rise to his highest potential. In fact, most children who never win at a game with their fathers will eventually lose interest in the game and will come to dislike the game intensely. No one likes to lose consistently.

We must never forget that the main purpose of play is to have fun. This does not mean that the child is not learning motor coordination, intellectual insights, skills he will need in adulthood, or athletic skills. All of these happen from time to time, but they are the by-product of play, not the purpose of play. Play is the time for laughing, a time for using the imagination, a time of creating worlds of fantasy.

A five-year-old daughter who is dressing a doll and explaining to her father that she is getting the doll ready to go to a party is expressing some of her own fantasy of the future. She may also be revealing much of what she understands about her parents' pursuits. It is in the context of play that we often hear our own values expressed by our children. We hear them say to dolls what we often say to them. I remember the little girl in a preschool class who said to her doll, "Now you sit right there in the corner until your father gets home." I was certain the mother would have been embarrassed if she had observed the behavior and words of her daughter. In play, we learn a lot about what goes on in the minds of our children.

5. *A loving father teaches his values.* In recent years, some have considered it inappropriate to teach values to one's children. The idea is that the child should be given the freedom to choose his or her own values. One mother refused to teach her children any of the religious songs that she had learned as a child because she did not want to predispose her child to any particular religious views. Such a philosophy assumes that children grow up in a vacuum and that at a certain age, they then choose the values that suit them. In my opinion, this is an utterly false assumption.

Children are influenced from their earliest days by all that is around them. Parents, teachers, caregivers, peers, the media—all have an impact upon the thinking and emotions of children. And, even if we consciously seek not to verbalize our values, we teach them by the way we live. In fact, our values determine our behavior. It is not difficult for a child to determine what is important to parents even if the parents give no verbal affirmations. For example, the father who goes to work daily without complaint teaches a child by that behavior that work is honorable and good and highly valued by the father. Without a word, the child learns the value of work.

The father who chooses to be a loving leader believes in his own values because he has found them to bring him a level of satisfaction, peace of mind, and purpose in life. This being the case, he desires to teach these values to his children. Values are simply those things in life to which we attach worth. Values are strongly held beliefs by which we order our lives. If we believe in the virtue of honesty, then we will seek to be honest in our dealing with others. If we believe in the virtue of hard work, then we will seek to give an honest day's work to our employer. If we believe in the virtue of kindness, it will be demonstrated in the way we treat and speak to our neighbors.

Of course, the teaching of values is a parental task borne both by mother and father. My emphasis here is on a father's intentionality in the formation of values, for if the father is silent in this area while the mother is vocal, the children may become insecure and even confused as to what the parents consider to be of value.

Since most of the values to which I am personally committed are rooted in the Bible, our live-in anthropologist often saw me sitting on the couch reading a Bible story to the children, letting them ask questions, and asking a few of my own. I am encouraged that my adult children have now chosen to live their lives within that framework of values.

Years ago I was complaining to my son, then in graduate school, about the number of parking tickets he had gotten in Cambridge, Massachusetts. His apartment was in nearby Arlington. He explained to me that in order to get a parking sticker for the city of Cambridge, one must live in Cambridge. "Some of my friends," he said, "lied and got stickers so that they could park in Cambridge without getting parking tickets. Somehow, I just didn't think that was honest, so I didn't do it. I would rather get a few parking tickets than lie." It was a stark reminder to me that honesty is sometimes costly, but I still believe that it is the best policy, and I am glad to see my son personalizing this virtue.

6. *A loving father provides for and protects his children.* This is the most basic level of fathering. Meeting the child's need for food, clothing, and shelter is the least a father can do for his offspring. I am appalled at the thousands of fathers today who choose to walk away from the mothers of their children and have no sense of responsibility for providing for the physical needs of these children. It is the most fundamental kind of rejection. No wonder many of the sons and daughters of such fathers grow up to lash out at others, in what is probably displaced anger toward their fathers.

I once had a friend who at fifty-plus lost the job that had brought him a good income for many years. In order to pay his basic bills, he laid aside his suit and tie and took a job stocking groceries in a local food store on the third shift. It was a totally new world for him, but he chose the high road of honest labor over the road of unemployment. After several weeks of this, I said to his daughter in his presence, "I want you to know what great respect I have for your father. I have known many men who have lost jobs and who have waited months for the right job to come along. Your father has not done that; he has taken the initiative to work in a very difficult situation in order to provide income for his family. I have great admiration for him." I could see the twinkle in her eye and knew that she too admired her father's choice.

A loving father will also protect his children. Yes, he will lock the doors at night. He may install an alarm system or at least set a big chair in front of the door at night. His action is, in my opinion, a simple act of human love that shows he wants the best for his children and is committed to protecting them from any who would do them ill.

A father who loves his children will make every effort to keep drugs and alcohol from destroying the lives of his offspring. He cannot ultimately control his children's behavior, including their choice to use alcohol or other drugs, but he will make every effort both by his model and by his teaching to keep them from such dangers. He will make time to talk to teachers, principals, and coaches or anyone else who might help him in the pursuit of protecting his children. One of his most fundamental desires is that his children live so that they can experience some of the joys that he has experienced in life.

7. *A loving father loves his children unconditionally.* Many fathers communicate these messages to their children: "I love you if you make good grades; I love you if you play sports well; I love you if you clean up your room; I love you if you feed the dog; I love you if you don't yell at me; I love you if you stay out of my way." Such love is payment for right behavior. True love has no conditions. "I am your father, and I am committed to your best interests no matter what. If you skip school, I still love you. I will do everything in my power to see that you attend school, but I will not reject you even if you do not live up to my expectations. My love will lead me to discipline you when I think that is appropriate. But because of my love, I will never reject you." That is the kind of love every child deserves from a father.

A CHILD'S-EYE VIEW: A FATHER'S ABSENCE

Since we discussed the importance of love in an earlier chapter, I will not belabor the point. But I do want to emphasize that the father's love is essential to the healthy emotional development of his children. Even children who have been deprived of a loving father have a dream of such a father. Listen to the following words written as an essay on the subject "What Is a Man?," written by a sixteen-year-old high school sophomore whose parents divorced when he was eight years old. His father left and never returned, and his stepdad was tyrannical, often saying to him such things as, "Shut up. You're worthless. Stupid. You'll never amount to anything." This is a boy who never really had a father, had never experienced the strong love of a true man, but had a vision of what a man is. Here is what he wrote:

A real man is kind.
A real man is caring.
A real man walks away from silly macho fights.
A real man helps his wife.
A real man helps his kids when they are sick.
A real man doesn't run from his problems.
A real man sticks to his word and keeps his promises.
A real man is honest.
A real man is not in trouble with the law.[4]

Here is one lonely boy's vision of a father who loves unconditionally.

CHAPTER TWELVE

For Wives Only:

THE FINE ART OF ENCOURAGING

It is my guess that most husbands fall somewhere between "perfect in every way" and "complete failure." You, as a wife, may have read the preceding chapters and wished your mate could live up to the description of a loving husband and father. Be encouraged: he can. But he can't do it without you.

I am not suggesting that you can change your husband. I am suggesting that you can be a positive influence in his life. The seven ideas I am going to present I have shared with hundreds of wives over the years in my counseling practice. They have been used and found effective by many.

MEN RESPOND POSITIVELY TO PRAISE

Jack was a tough man in the business world, but in my office he was crying. "I don't understand it. In the business world, I am respected. People come to me for advice and I am often affirmed, but at home, all I get is criticism. My wife's comments to me are always critical. You would think I was an absolute failure. I know I am not, but I think that is the way she perceives me." Later, as I talked to his wife, Liz, I found out that she agreed that he was a good husband and father—but there were a few areas in which she strongly believed that he needed growth. And she was determined to bring these to his attention.

The problem was that what Liz considered suggestions, Jack saw as criticisms. Her efforts to encourage growth had backfired. Instead of making positive changes, he resented her. His motivation to change was depleted.

The fact is that none of us responds well to constant criticism. On the other hand, all of us respond well to expressions of praise and appreciation. From the smallest child to the oldest adult, when our fan club applauds us, we try harder. The child who falls when learning to walk will be encouraged to try again by the adult who cheers him or her on. The husband who wants desperately to feel good about himself will be encouraged to try harder when his wife praises his efforts.

Thus, if you want to motivate your husband toward growth, focus on the things he is doing well and praise him. And *please don't wait for perfection before you offer praise.* Commend him for effort even if his performance is not up to your expectation. The fastest way to influence quality performance is to express appreciation for past performance. Perhaps you're asking, "But if I praise him for mediocrity, will it not stifle growth?" The answer is a resounding no. Your praise urges him on to greater accomplishments. Conversely, if you do not express appreciation for his efforts along the way, he may conclude that it is unimportant to you and cease to be motivated. My challenge to you is to look for things your husband is doing right and praise him. Praise him in private, praise him in front of the children, praise him in front of your parents and his parents, praise him in front of his peers. Then stand back and watch him go for the gold.

REQUESTS . . . NOT DEMANDS

None of us likes to be controlled, and demands are efforts at controlling. "If you don't mow the lawn this afternoon, then I am going to mow it." I wouldn't make such a demand unless you want to be the permanent lawn cutter. It is far more effective to say, "Do you know what would really make me happy?" and wait until he asks "What?" Then tell him, "If you would mow the grass this afternoon." You might add, "I would even be willing to help if you would like." (Don't add the last offer unless you are sincere!)

Let me illustrate by applying the principle to you. How would you feel if your husband said, "You haven't baked me any cookies since the baby was born. I guess I'll be eating Chips Ahoy for eighteen more years"? Now, doesn't that motivate you to run into the kitchen and start whipping up some cookie dough? Fat chance. But imagine that he says to you, "You know what I'd really like to have? Some of your chocolate chip cookies—the ones with little nuts in them. Just sometime when you get a chance . . ." Chances are, he'll be munching on warm cookies before the week is over. Why? We all respond more positively to requests than to demands.

When you want to motivate your husband to spend more time with the children, don't say, "If you don't start spending time with the kids, you're gonna miss out on their lives. They're going to be gone before we know it." Far better to share your desire in terms of a request. "Would it be possible for you to play online Scrabble with Anna tonight? She had such fun the last time you guys played." I'm not suggesting that your husband will do everything you request. I am suggesting that he will be far more responsive to your requests than to your demands.

The more specific your request, the easier it is for your husband to respond. Requests like "I wish we could have more fun" or "I wish you would spend more time with Josh" are too general to be effective.

Far better to request that the two of you go to a movie or that he work with Josh on a school project.

Perhaps you would find it helpful to list the six characteristics of a loving husband and the seven characteristics of a loving father, and under each of these write one or two specific requests that you think would enhance your husband's role as a loving leader. Please don't give him your list of requests all at once, but select from your list one request per week. Throw in a little praise along with the request, and you may well see your husband responding much more positively to your desires.

MEN NEED LOVE TOO

It sounds simple, but it is easy to forget: men desperately need emotional love. The person a man would most like to love him is his wife and, in fact, if he genuinely feels loved by his wife the world looks bright and he will reach his highest potential. If, on the other hand, his love tank is empty and he does not feel loved by his wife, the world will look dark and he will sink to the lowest level. Thus, few things are more important in motivating your husband to positive growth than consistently meeting his need for love. In an earlier section, we discussed the five love languages and the importance of learning to speak your spouse's primary love language. I will not repeat that information here, except to say that few things are more important than discovering and speaking your husband's primary love language. If you speak his language consistently, you will meet his need for emotional love. With a full love tank, he is far more motivated in his efforts to be a loving husband and father.

My file is filled with letters like the following:

Dr. Chapman, I am compelled to write you and say thanks for your book *The Five Love Languages*. It has changed my marriage in the most dramatic way. My husband and I had been drifting along in a relationship. We were feeling distant and our conflicts were coming more frequently. A friend gave me your book and upon reading it, I discovered I had not been speaking my husband's primary love language for many years, nor had he been speaking mine. I suggested he read the book but his schedule is busy and he didn't read it for several weeks. I was disappointed but decided to practice what I had learned. So I started speaking his language on a regular basis. His whole attitude toward me began to change. When he asked why I had been so different lately, I told him it was because of the book I had read on the five love languages. He decided that maybe he should read the book. He did and we discussed it. He acknowledged that he had not been speaking my primary language either and the next week, I saw a distinct change in his response to me. Now we both have full love tanks and our marriage has never been better. I just wanted to thank you for the book and to let you know that I am sharing it with all my friends.

Sincerely,
Beverly

Beverly is not unique. Love is the most powerful weapon for good in the world, and when a wife chooses to love her husband and learns how to express that love in his primary love language, the husband's love tank begins to fill and his attitude begins to change. It does make a profound difference in his level of motivation to work on his marriage and parenting skills.

MEETING ONE ANOTHER'S NEEDS

In many ways, marriage is a mutual aid society. Both of us are needy creatures. That is what drew us together. The bottom line is that men and women were made for each other. Our differences were designed to complement. When marriage is healthy, the husband's needs are met by an intimate relationship with his wife and her needs are met by an intimate, loving relationship with him.

In his book *His Needs, Her Needs*, Willard Harley states that the husband's top five needs are (1) sexual fulfillment, (2) recreational companionship, (3) an attractive spouse, (4) domestic support, and (5) admiration; whereas the wife's top five needs are (1) affection, (2) conversation, (3) honesty and openness, (4) financial support, and (5) family commitment.[1]

This does not mean that all husbands and wives fit into a neat category. It does mean that our needs are almost always different.

The important thing is to discover your husband's basic needs and ways in which you can meet them. Your meeting those needs will enhance his sense of self-worth and fulfillment. In the previous chapters, we have said that discovering and meeting his wife's needs is one of the characteristics of a loving husband. Now I am suggesting that if you want to encourage your husband in this pursuit, you may best do it by a conscious effort to meet his needs. When each of us focuses on meeting the other's needs, we both become winners. This is marriage at its best. When our needs are met, our children not only have a model of a successful marriage, they are the beneficiaries of the overflow. Husbands and wives whose emotional needs are met by each other are far more effective in parenting.

WHY HUSBANDS GET DEFENSIVE

I am often asked by wives, "Why does my husband get so defensive?" Megan said, "All I have to do is mention that the grass needs mowing and he goes ballistic. Why does he get so bent out of shape?" Allyson said, "We're driving down the road. Everything is fine. I notice that he is going seventy miles per hour. I remind him that the speed limit is fifty-five, and he starts yelling and screaming. I don't understand his behavior." Both Megan and Allyson are experiencing defensive reactions by their husbands. Such behavior seems totally incomprehensible to them. The fact is that both husbands are revealing something about themselves. Defensiveness always reveals the inner self.

Defensiveness is my reaction when someone touches my self-esteem. When something threatens my sense of self-worth, I will have a defensive response. Megan and Allyson's husbands are revealing a self-esteem hot spot. In their histories, something has tied mowing the lawn and speeding to their self-esteem. Perhaps it was a father who constantly was on his son's back about mowing the lawn, who told him what a worthless son he was because he had to be pressured to mow the grass weekly. Perhaps it was a series of speeding tickets in adolescence that communicated "You are a poor driver," so when their wives mention the lawn or the speed limit, they have defensive reactions. Or perhaps the problem is more general; her comment sounds to him like criticism, and he feels attacked.

We do not know what these emotional hot spots are until we touch one of them. It would be a good idea to make a list of all your husband's defensive reactions. Note what you said or did and how he responded. You will begin to discover these hot spots, and, in due time with reflection, you will find out why he is responding defensively. Anytime you do or say something that stimulates a negative message about his self-esteem, he will be defensive. His defensiveness is revealing to you the self-depreciating messages recorded in the inner self. When you gain this insight, you will more readily understand why he is defensive. Without this understanding, his defensive reactions will likely stimulate angry emotions inside of you or bewilderment at his behavior. With this insight, you are equipped to learn a more constructive response.

The key to learning how to lessen his defensive reactions is learning to communicate your concerns in a way that will not strike at his self-esteem. For example, let's look at Bill's defensiveness about

Megan's request that he mow the lawn. If he tends to get defensive anytime she mentions the lawn, she can assume this is in some way tied to his self-esteem. Therefore, in an open conversation with him on an evening when they are not in conflict, she may say something like the following. "Bill, I want to discuss something with you that I think will make our lives better. I've noticed that when I mention mowing the grass to you, your natural response is to be defensive. I'm assuming that something in your past related to mowing the grass is causing this defensiveness. It's obvious that you find it offensive. I hope you know that my intention is not to anger you, so I would like to find a better way to handle this. My concern is simply that the yard look presentable. I'm not trying to put you down or to criticize you. You're a wonderful husband, and most of the time the yard looks nice. Would it be better if I wrote you a note when I feel the yard needs attention rather than verbalizing it to you? Or would you prefer that when I think the yard needs attention, I should do it myself? Or would you prefer that I hire someone to do it? Or do you have other suggestions?" Chances are, Bill will be responsive to what she is saying, and together they can find a way for her to express her concern without stimulating defensiveness in him.

Seek to learn from your husband's defensive reactions. If he chooses to read this chapter, perhaps you can discuss the whole concept of defensiveness with each other and both of you can gain insight into the other's self-esteem hot spots. Such understanding will create deeper intimacy between the two of you as well as lead you to less defensive ways of relating to each other.

MEN, SEX, AND EMOTIONS

Her face was red. Her voice was desperate. "Dr. Chapman, what is wrong with my husband? Every time I turn around, it's sex, sex, sex. I think that's all he has on his mind. Isn't marriage more than sex?"

How many wives have shared these sentiments through the years? In the section on marital intimacy, we discussed the differences between males and females sexually. For the wife who desires to stimulate growth in her husband as a loving leader, it is important to remember these differences.

The male sexual drive is rooted in his anatomy. The gonads are continually producing sperm cells. These are stored along with seminal fluid in the seminal vesicles. When the seminal vesicles are full, there is a physical push for release. This creates the heightened male sex drive. There is nothing comparable to this in the female. She has her menstrual period, and this certainly affects her sexual desires, but there is nothing physically that builds up within, pushing her to have sexual release. Her desire for sexual intimacy is more rooted in her emotions. When she feels emotionally loved and close to her husband, she is far more likely to want to be sexually intimate. But when she does not feel loved and cared for, she may have little interest in the sexual part of marriage unless that is the one place where she does feel loved.

Understanding and responding to this difference may greatly affect the husband's attitude toward his wife. When the husband's sexual appetite is unmet, he tends to become irritable and withdrawn or critical. When the sexual need is met, he tends to be more relaxed and calm. If the husband has made considerable progress in developing the characteristics of a loving leader as described in this section, chances are his wife will find it easy to be sexually responsive to him, and their sexual relationship will be a positive experience for both. But if he is deficient as a loving leader, this may be an area of serious struggle.

As I have encouraged the husband to love his wife unconditionally, so here I must encourage the wife to love her husband unconditionally. In the sexual area, this may mean going against your emotions. Recognizing the nature of his sexual need and desiring to take the initiative in loving him, she initiates sexual intimacy as an expression of love. Meeting his sexual need on a regular basis creates an atmosphere where she can communicate to him how to more effectively meet her need by making specific requests of him. In this loving context, he is likely to respond to her requests and, in so doing, meet her emotional needs.

If, on the other hand, she chooses to use sex as a weapon against him and withholds sex until he yields to her demands, she has created a battlefield rather than a loving relationship. In such battles, there are no winners. Battles tend to escalate until each party has destroyed the other. A healthy marriage is created by genuine efforts to meet each other's needs. The wife who takes initiative in the sexual area is having a positive influence upon her husband's efforts to develop his own loving leadership skills.

CONFRONTATION CAN BE LOVING

In most marriages, the six suggestions I have made in this chapter will have a positive influence upon the husband's attitude. Praise tends to beget praise; requests tend to be honored. When his needs are met, he finds it easier to respond to her needs. Love begets love, and when defensiveness is understood and defused, life flows smoothly. When sexual needs are met, he is free to focus on other family issues. But I would be unfair if I gave wives the impression that if they will follow these six guidelines, their husbands will always continue to grow as loving husbands and fathers. There are times when husbands must be confronted about irresponsible behavior.

Confrontation is not a negative word. In fact, it is an act of love if it is done with the right attitude. Let's return to the three wives we met in chapter 10. Elaine's husband has not held a steady job in ten years, and when he is out of work he spends his time watching TV and working out at the local gym. Elaine has carried the financial load for their entire marriage. I do not know if her husband would have responded differently had she applied the six suggestions in this chapter. I do know that if his pattern of irresponsibility persists in spite of her efforts, then confrontation would be a loving act.

If Elaine had said to him early in the marriage, "I love you very much. It is my desire to have an intimate relationship with you. I have noticed that in every job you've had, you've found fault with the job or with the people with whom you work. This time, rather than quitting the job, I want to request that you talk with someone about the situation and try to find a different way to handle the problem." She may even suggest a specific counselor or pastor.

If he refuses this request and repeats the pattern of walking off the job, then it is time for her to express tough love and inform him that she will not continue to pay the bills while he watches TV and works out at the gym. And she must take appropriate steps to show him that she is serious. The only way to break an irresponsible pattern is to hold him accountable for his actions. As long as he is able to have his cake and eat it too, it is not likely that his work patterns will change. Tough love runs the risk of losing him, but it also holds the potential of stimulating growth and giving her a more responsible husband.

Tracy was the wife whose husband worked regularly and provided for the financial needs of the family but was an excessive controller. He considered her ideas useless, and he would not tolerate her questions about his behavior and would become belligerent when she questioned any of his actions. Tracy was living in bondage to a domineering husband.

If the loving efforts we have discussed in this chapter did not stimulate positive change in her husband, then there is a place for her to say to him with kindness and firmness, "I love you too much to let you destroy yourself and me. In many ways, you are a wonderful husband. But in the matter of control, you are destroying both of us. Until you are willing to discuss the problem with me and with a counselor, I will not be able to live with you until we get help. I am fully willing to work on our marriage and I believe we have a marriage worth saving, but I cannot do it alone. I must have your cooperation." Again, such confrontation runs the risk of creating the crisis of separation, but sometimes a crisis is necessary in order to stimulate positive growth. Tracy is not abandoning her husband in such action; she is, in fact, loving him enough to take a risk.

Becky was the wife whose husband was passive in all areas except his vocation and his computer. For six years their bedroom had needed painting. When the children's bicycles needed repair, it would be months before he responded. Her first recourse, as with Elaine and Tracy, should be to try the six suggestions we have made in this chapter; but if, over a period of time, these fail to stimulate growth in her husband, there is a place for confrontation. She might say to him, "I love you very much. I appreciate deeply the fact that you work regularly and contribute financially to our family. But I want you to know that I cannot continue to live with your passive spirit. I do not expect you to be Superman, but I do need you to do at least one project around the house every week. We are paying to have the yard mowed, and that is fine. But there are other things that need your attention. I'm asking for your help. I do not wish to overwhelm you, but I do wish to see a change. If I cannot rely on you to take initiative to accomplish one project per week in our household, I will have to find someone I can rely on that I can hire to do these tasks. If that doesn't seem reasonable to you, then I am willing to discuss it with you and a counselor. I want more than anything to be a good wife to you, and I am open to your suggestions, but it must be a two-way street."

If such confrontation seems to be harsh and threatening, let me remind you that this is the last resort. When you have tried the power of praise, when you have made specific requests, when you have loved him unconditionally and sought to meet his needs, when you have sought to understand his defensiveness and find ways to build up his self-esteem, when you have sought to respond to him sexually, and he still is involved in irresponsible behavior, it is time for strong, firm, loving confrontation. Such action is, in fact, the most loving thing a wife can do. To enable your husband to be irresponsible for thirty years is not a service to him, nor to your children. When a husband who has a loving, supporting wife who has taken the steps suggested in this chapter realizes that he is in danger of losing her, he may be highly motivated to change his thinking and his behavior. Her confrontation has created a crisis to which he must respond. Many husbands have looked back upon such a crisis and been thankful that their wives had the courage to love them enough to force them to take constructive action. Confrontation can indeed be a strong act of love.

Even in confrontation, a wife cannot make her husband change. Change is a choice only the individual can make. But because marriage is such an intimate relationship, the wife's behavior can greatly influence the husband. I believe the suggestions I have made in this chapter have the potential for encouraging many husbands to develop positive skills in becoming loving husbands and fathers. In your efforts to be a positive influence on your husband, remember that the goal is not perfection; the goal is growth. Be encouraged when your husband takes positive steps, and remember, growth takes time. He may not be all that you wish, but if he is growing, the potential is unlimited.

For more information on how you can cultivate leadership skills to love and lead your family well, see the code on page 177 to access the Family Adventure Guide at **www.5lovelanguages .com/5traits**. This guide is to help put into practice the healthy traits discussed in this book. You'll find a number of assessments, things to think about, and opportunities for deeper discussion.

Epilogue

It will be obvious to all that this is not a book to be read. It is a book to be experienced. I have told you what I believe to be the five traits of a truly healthy family. In doing so, I have invited you into my own family. You have not slept in the basement room as did John, our live-in anthropologist, but I hope that you have sensed something of what has gone on in our family through the years.

I have not written as a detached ethnographer describing the five traits of a loving family. I have written rather with the passion of one who is deeply concerned about the well-being of a rising generation. Over the last forty-five years, I have worked closely enough with people to know that the principles explained in this book are essential to producing a healthy family. Increasing numbers of young people have not seen a demonstration of a loving family and consequently have little idea of where to begin. It is my desire that this book will serve as a starting place. For the young couples who sincerely want to establish a loving family, I hope that this volume will serve not only to give a paradigm of principles but will also serve as a workbook giving practical instructions on how to develop these traits within your own family.

The five traits I have described are as old as humanity itself. They have guided families of many cultures over thousands of years, but they are in grave danger of being lost today, in an era when we have lost society's consensus over the importance of the family unit.

I am fully aware that for those who have grown up in dysfunctional families and are now trying to establish their own family, the ideas I have discussed in this book may be overwhelming. That is why I emphasized earlier that this is a book to be experienced, not a book to be read. It is my desire that after a cursory reading, couples will go back to the sections where they have the greatest need for growth and use the practical suggestions for building these characteristics into their own family. It is a book I hope you will revisit often when you have the sense that something is missing in your family relationships. It is also my desire that the book will be used by counselors, educators, and other caregivers as a tool for stimulating discussion and action regarding marriage and family matters.

When John came to observe our family so many years ago, I had no idea the impact it would have on his life or ours. When I asked him years later, "What is your overall assessment of the value of the year you spent with us?" his answer was all the reward I could ever want. Here, in part, is what he said:

> Then and looking back now, I just really enjoyed it. It was a very affirming place for me. A safe environment, stable; at a time in my life when my own home was none of those. There was not good communication in my home growing up either between my parents or between either of my parents and me. There was not mutual respect. There was dysfunction virtually all the way around. When I came into your home, I began for the first time to have a model to observe what it could be like. . . .
>
> I think that was of tremendous value to me in later being able to respect my own wife and appreciate her as an individual and to be able to talk through things. I don't know what I would have done if I had not lived in your home before I went into

marriage. I shudder to think. It really gave me a very important transition into my life as a husband and later as a father.

In closing, it is my sincere desire that you will find in this book a light that guides you toward building the family you've always wanted. It is the multiplying of healthy families that produces a healthy society, and it is healthy, functioning societies that create a world of harmony. What happens to your family does make a difference—not only to you and your children but to the thousands of young observers who are in search of the family they always wanted.

A Word from Shelley and Derek

"THE PLACE I GET TO KNOW GOD"

As I think about the impact of growing up in my family, two ideas recur. One is that family is labor. Not in the cold sense of all work, no play, but in that to make it work, everyone must work and invest in the whole. The other key seed planted in me that continues to bear good fruit is the sense of a lack of separation between one's spiritual life and one's family life. I think the idea is this: the family is an extension and expression of the church. My spiritual life, growing up, was intimately connected to my family life. Both of these concepts have stuck with me and given me a good foundation for beginning my own family.

The concept of labor as a motivation is unattractive to much of my generation. But the reality is that marriage is labor, and in many ways allows us to fellowship with Christ's suffering. Again—not that it is all labor, but I think one needs to enter family life thinking *sacrifice* and *service* to make it work.

Marriage and family are meant to help us know and love God even more. I saw this "wedding" of spiritual life and family life growing up, so I did not struggle to reconcile them later on. For me, marriage and family are the core place I meet and get to know God. This is a radical concept in contemporary society, which tends to separate God and family into two almost opposing categories. So I am thankful I grew up seeing both the labor and the spirituality of being married and of building family.

—Derek Chapman

"WHAT BREATHING IS TO THE BODY"

My childhood experiences left me with a profound respect for intimacy. I was acutely aware that good communication (listening and talking) was the only way to have intellectual, emotional, social, physical, and spiritual intimacy. Healthy communication is to marriage and family what breathing is to the body—essential. John and I cultivated our relationship for thirteen years before we married. (Both of us were in medical school and completing our residency programs.) Even then, I fully expected the first years of our marriage to be difficult. Why else would my home as a child be so busy with couples coming for counseling? (This intimate communication must be HARD work.) I was surprised to find out that communication skills learned as a child, and used during courting, led to days full of intimacy with my mate.

Our children now enjoy one-on-one time with each of us at the end of the day as we read stories, talk about the events of the day, and pray. Our desire is that they will learn to communicate intimately within the family and that this will open their lives to healthy relationships. I reflect often on the hours I spent with my parents at the close of each day and how that prepared me for a healthy marriage and family. For that I am deeply grateful.

—Shelley Chapman McGuirt, MD

Acknowledgments

The word *family* implies husband, wife, and children. For us, family means Gary, Karolyn, Shelley, and Derek. Our extended family includes son-in-law John, daughter-in-law Amy, and grandchildren: Davy Grace and Elliott Isaac. Inasmuch as this book, to some extent, exposes our family in its formative years, I want to express my sincere gratitude to my family for allowing me to tell something of our journey.

I am especially grateful for the role Derek played in reading the manuscript and making insightful suggestions, as well as for his creative expression of memories and emotions in the poems that appear throughout the book.

Genuine appreciation goes to John Nesbitt, our live-in anthropologist. He was kind enough to give me considerable time reflecting on the year he spent with our family many years ago.

I am deeply indebted to Tricia Kube, my administrative assistant for a decade and a half, who computerized the manuscript and made many helpful suggestions; along with Betsey Newenhuyse and Avrie Roberts of Moody Publishers for their expert editorial help.

Last, but certainly not least, I want to express appreciation to the scores of persons whose stories appear on these pages. Names and places are of course changed to protect their privacy, but their willingness to share their pain and joy with me has kept this volume rooted in real life.

DOWNLOAD FREE RESOURCE

For the free online Family Adventure Guide, visit:

www.5lovelanguages.com/5traits

Access code: 4F4M1LY

This family guide is to help identify the current habits within your family and equip you to apply the five healthy traits discussed in this book. These exercises will hopefully help you strengthen your family, and, perhaps, understand yourself a little better.

Notes

PROLOGUE—AN OUTSIDER IN THE FAMILY

1. Edith Schaeffer, *What Is a Family?* (Grand Rapids: Revell, 1975), 211.

CHAPTER TWO—HOW FAMILIES SERVE

1. William J. Bennett, *The Book of Virtues* (New York: Simon & Schuster, 1993).
2. Philip Yancey, "Humility's Many Faces," *Christianity Today*, December 4, 2000, christianitytoday.com/ct/2000/december4/37.96.html.
3. John 13:14–15, 17.
4. Matthew 20:26.

CHAPTER THREE—OUR LONGING FOR CLOSENESS

1. Genesis 2:23.
2. Gary D. Chapman, *The 5 Love Languages: The Secret to Love That Lasts* (Chicago: Northfield Publishing, 2015).
3. Genesis 2:25.

CHAPTER FOUR—FIVE STEPS TO INTIMACY

1. Victor Hugo, *Les Misérables*, trans. Lee Fahnestock and Norman MacAfee (New York: Penguin, 1987).

CHAPTER FIVE—TALKING, DOING, LOVING

1. Bobbie Gee, "A Legacy of Love," in *Chicken Soup for the Soul*, eds. Jack Canfield and Mark Victor Hansen (Deerfield Beach, FL: Health Communications, 1993), 117–18.
2. Gary Chapman and Ross Campbell, *The 5 Love Languages of Children* (Chicago: Northfield Publishing, 1997).
3. Ross Campbell, *How to Really Love Your Child* (Wheaton, IL: Victor Books, 1980).
4. For a fuller explanation of the love language concept and how it relates to marriage as well as to children, see Gary Chapman, *The 5 Love Languages: The Secret to Love That Lasts* (Chicago: Northfield Publishing, 2015) and Chapman and Campbell, *The 5 Love Languages of Children*.

CHAPTER SIX—THE CHALLENGE OF CREATIVE TEACHING

1. Deuteronomy 6:7.
2. This quote is attributed to Dr. Graham Blaine.

CHAPTER SEVEN—THE CHALLENGE OF CONSISTENT TRAINING

1. Karl Menninger, quoted in Herbert V. Prochnow and Herbert V. Prochnow, Jr., *5100 Quotations for Speakers and Writers* (Grand Rapids: Baker Books, 1992), 380.
2. This quote is attributed to Abraham Lincoln.

CHAPTER NINE—THE GIFT OF HONOR

1. Wayne E. Warner, *1,000 Stories and Quotations of Famous People* (Grand Rapids: Baker Books, 1975), 64.

CHAPTER ELEVEN—WHAT FATHERS DO FOR THEIR FAMILIES

1. Stephanie Kramer, "US Has World's Highest Rate of Children Living in Single-Parent Households," Pew Research, December 12, 2019, https://www.pewresearch.org/fact-tank/2019/12/12/u-s-children-more-likely-than-children-in-other-countries-to-live-with-just-one-parent/.

2. Robert Bly, "The Hunger for the King in a Time with No Father," in *Fathers: Sons and Daughters*, ed. Charles S. Scull (Los Angeles: Jeremy P. Tarcher, 1992), 60.

3. James L. Schaller, *The Search for Lost Fathering* (Grand Rapids: Revell, 1995), 16.

4. William F. Hodges, *Interventions for Children of Divorce: Custody, Access, and Psychotherapy* (New York: Wiley, 1991), 1.

CHAPTER TWELVE—FOR WIVES ONLY: THE FINE ART OF ENCOURAGING

1. Willard F. Harley Jr., *His Needs, Her Needs: Building an Affair-Proof Marriage* (Grand Rapids: Revell, 1986).

Gary Chapman has helped millions of marriages. Now let him teach the 5 Love Languages® to your teens and kids!

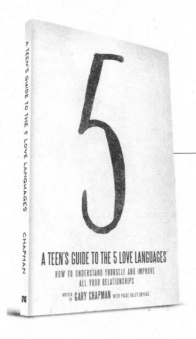

Derived from the original #1 *New York Times* bestseller, *A Teen's Guide to the 5 Love Languages* is the first-ever edition written just to teens, for teens, and with a teen's world in mind. It guides emerging adults in discovering and understanding their own love languages as well as how to best express love to others.

978-0-8024-1435-9
also available as an eBook

Gary Chapman and Rick Osborne help children learn about the importance of love in this wonderfully imaginative and classically illustrated children's hardcover book featuring four-color illustrations (with hidden details!) by Wilson Williams Jr., and based on Gary's bestselling *The 5 Love Languages*. FREE mobile app available.

978-0-8024-0358-2
also available as an eBook

NORTHFIELD
PUBLISHING

Supporting Families with Hope, Understanding, and Love

Blended families face unique challenges, and sadly, good intentions aren't always enough. With *Building Love Together in Blended Families* you can begin using the five love languages to help unite your stepfamily. With the right strategies and smart work, you can build a family that's stronger and healthier together.

978-0-8024-1905-7
Also available as an eBook

In this wise, warm, practical guide, you'll learn how the five love languages can help strengthen your marriage and family life—whatever your needs. Sharing dozens of stories from parents of children with special needs, the authors teach you how to love every member of your family without exhausting yourself.

978-0-8024-1862-3
Also available as an eBook

NORTHFIELD
PUBLISHING

Intentional resources for adding love, meaning, and adventure to your family days

You're a committed parent. You love your kids. But even on good days, you can feel tired. We've all been there. *Family Time*, born out of the authors' own experiences and desires to love their children well, is an invaluable resource of activities incorporating each of the five love languages.

978-0-8024-2971-1 | also available as an eBook

Whether it's a family pillow fight, a lip-sync competition, or Toilet Paper Olympics, give your family the gift of lifelong memories while having fun, connecting spiritually, and speaking each other's love languages. Enjoy all the benefits of the quality time you dreamed of without all the pressure of advanced planning.

978-0-8024-1939-2 | also available as an eBook

Has Technology Taken Over Your Home?

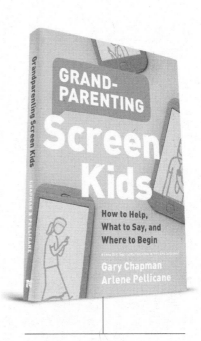

Today, children spend more time interacting with screens and less time playing outside or interacting with family. *Screen Kids* will empower you to make positive changes. This newly revised edition features the latest research and interactive assessments, so you can best confront the issues technology creates in your home.

978-0-8024-2220-0
Also available as eBook and audiobook

Grandparenting Screen Kids is the perfect resource for any grandparent who is concerned about screen time. This guide will help you understand this different world of iPads, YouTube, and video games. Technology isn't going anywhere, and your grandkids need you more than ever to guide them in ways that computers can't.

978-0-8024-2070-1
Also available as eBook and audiobook

NORTHFIELD
PUBLISHING